THAI
COOKING

THAI COOKING

FROM THE
SIAM CUISINE
RESTAURANT

**Kwanruan Aksomboon, Somchai Aksomboon,
and Diana Hiranaga**

North Atlantic Books, Berkeley, California

ACKNOWLEDGMENTS

I would like to give special thanks to the copy editor Jessie Wood, the indexer Elinor Lindheimer, my friends, Jenny Choy and Carol Bloomstein, and to Pete Clemono of the University of California Botanical Gardens.

Thai Cooking from the Siam Cuisine Restaurant

Copyright © 1989 by Kwanruan Aksomboon, Somchai Aksomboon, and Diana Hiranaga

ISBN 1–55643–074–4 (paperback)
ISBN 1–55643–074–2 (cloth)

Published by North Atlantic Books
       2800 Woolsey Street
       Berkeley, California 94705

Cover photo: Thai Chicken Soup
Cover and book design by Paula Morrison
Typeset by Campaigne and Somit Typography

Thai Cooking from the Siam Cuisine Restaurant is sponsored by the Society for the Study of Native Arts and Sciences, a nonprofit educational corporation whose goals are to develop an ecological and crosscultural perspective linking various scientific, social, and artistic fields; to nurture a holistic view of arts, sciences, humanities, and healing; and to publish and distribute literature on the relationship of body, mind, and nature.

Fourth Printing

Table of Contents

The Restaurant and Its Owners

It was my love of hole-in-the-wall restaurants that gave me my first taste of Thai food. The place was the Siam Café with its twenty-two seats around a C-shaped counter. It had no tables and was brightly lit with bare fluorescent tubes. Looking over the counter and through the doorway into the compact kitchen, customers could chat with the cooks and owners, Somchai and Kwan Aksomboon. It was so easy and comfortable to talk with them, it was like being at home.

But it was the food that caught and held our attention. My husband Terry and I soon became addicted to the fragrant combination of pungent spices simmered in coconut milk and the stir-fried chicken spiked with aromatic basil and fiery chili peppers. Even though we always left the restaurant with full stomachs, we inevitably craved more, as though each meal was a dose of some habit-forming drug. We just could not get enough of it. The flavors, aromas, and textures were so phenomenal that we ate there three or four times a week. The fact that the prices were so reasonable only impelled us to return for more. Two people could eat a complete dinner, including soup, a main dish, rice, and vegetable for under $7.00. It was truly an incredible find—even in 1978.

The Siam Café was Somchai and Kwan's first restaurant in the San Francisco Bay Area, but it was their second venture here in the United States. Somchai came to United States in 1972 and Kwan in 1973 with her daughter, Ajchara, and son, Kenneth. They met in Arlington, Texas, where they married and opened a Thai restaurant. The restaurant proved to be a source of frustration. Thai food was new to the American palate and Somchai and Kwan felt that the people of Texas were just not ready for this exotic cuisine. After twenty-one months they sold their share of the restaurant to their partner and moved to California.

They set up housekeeping in Berkeley and worked at several restaurants in the San Francisco Bay Area, where people were decidedly more adventurous toward different foods. In 1978, they decided to start another restaurant and within a few weeks, Siam Café opened in a small vacant diner on San Pablo Avenue in Berkeley.

Except for an occasional employee, the café was completely family-operated. While Somchai and Kwan cooked and washed dishes, Ajchara, age 12, waited on customers and bussed tables. Kenneth, age 6, sat at the end of the counter studying, playing, or talking to customers. They served breakfast, lunch, and dinner, emphasizing mainly Chinese food with a few Thai specialties. Customers familiar with Thai Cuisine often came in to request dishes that did not appear on the menu. They were usually told to come back the next day, when they would inevitably get exactly what they had asked for. As a result the menu grew to include more and more Thai dishes.

Alcohol was never served at the café. If you wanted beer to cool down the heat of the chili peppers, you had to bring your own.

The Siam Café was the first Thai restaurant in the East Bay, and it proved to be very successful. Within nine months they had sold their business and were in search of a new, larger location. The site they chose was the old Harry's Bar on University Avenue in Berkeley. So in December of 1979, they opened the doors of the new, greatly expanded Siam Cuisine, which also happened to coincide with the birth of their son, Wonchalurm.

In the beginning, business was slow and tentative. My husband and I were still going there two or three times a week, still enjoying our familiar favorite dishes and discovering all the new mouth-watering flavors on the expanded menu. But there were times when we were the only ones in the restaurant. All the black-and-white-clad waiters were at our service, eagerly anticipating and meeting our every need. However, on those evenings when one of the employees had not shown up for work, or it was busier than they had expected, we often found ourselves washing dishes, serving customers, or bussing tables. So much for a nice quiet meal.

These days, of course, Siam Cuisine runs very smoothly, and I know of no other customer who has been asked to wash dishes. The restaurant continues to improve, though, in all sorts of ways. Even the interior has changed. The old Harry's Bar was a dim cocktail lounge with red vinyl booths and a gas fireplace in the center. In 1986 the restaurant was totally remodeled, inside and out, with blond wood planking and light grey carpeting, giving it a clean, light, welcoming feeling.

The exterior now has a tall, steep roofline with gables that curve up at the ends, typical of Thai architecture. At the long L-shaped bar, housed beneath the steep open ceiling, waiting customers can enjoy any of twenty beers or fourteen wines; they no longer have to bring their own.

Somchai and Kwan's responsibilities have also changed. Their duties shift and overlap, but basically Somchai manages the restaurant and makes sure the dining room runs smoothly while Kwan commands the kitchen, overseeing the cooks and organizing the food preparation.

Ethnically Somchai is Chinese, but he was born and raised in Thailand. Like many people of other ethnic groups in Thailand, he and his family have assimilated Thai foods as an integral part of their cuisine. Having had the good fortune of being influenced by the flavors and spices of both countries, Somchai cooks both Chinese and Thai dishes. He also possesses the innate ability to join these flavors and spices to create tantalizing new dishes. Somchai's food savvy coupled with his warm, friendly personality and his keen business sense have given him the versatility needed to run a restaurant.

Kwan rarely cooked in Thailand. It was always her mother or father who prepared the meals. If she didn't like what was being cooked at home, she could always find something to her liking down the street at the local marketplace. In the United States she found no street vendors or Thai restaurants to satisfy her taste buds so she wrote to her mother, asking for recipes. Instead of sending her the exact proportions, her mother sent lists of ingredients. Kwan learned how to make each dish by trial and error from her memory of what the food should taste like, experimenting always to get the right combination of flavors. This "learning by doing" is typical of the Thai method of cooking.

The kitchen of Siam Cuisine is a beehive of activity. At the stove the cooks are sautéing, grilling, frying, and setting up each dish; at another station the food preparers are pounding, grinding, measuring, and mixing. Still others are boning, juicing, and chopping, just to keep up with the volume of raw materials needed by the cooks. All these components are brought together once a customer orders.

Stocking a restaurant the size of Siam Cuisine is a monumental task. Somchai goes to Chinatown daily to buy fish and other perishable items, while Kwan handpicks each Blue Lake green bean and other vegetables at the local produce markets. All the dry spices, preserved foods, condiments, sauces, noodles, rice, and beer must be ordered directly from the suppliers. What they can't buy, they grow. Behind the restaurant and at home in their greenhouse, they have planters filled with: Thai basil, lemon basil, dark opal basil, and holy basil; several types of mint and chili peppers; coriander; lemon grass; Chinese celery; and Kaffir lime trees, in addition to a variety of other exotic herbs and spices not otherwise available.

To give you an idea of the volume of food that passes through Siam Cuisine, here is a typical weekly shopping list of the most frequently consumed items.

Bean sprouts: 70 pounds

Blue Lake green beans: 25 pounds

Garlic: 40 pounds

Jalapeño chili peppers: 30 pounds

Thai basil: 8 pounds

Coconut milk: 100 gallons

Beef: 180 pounds

Chicken: 800 pounds

Calamari: 180 pounds

Whole fish: 105 pounds

Fish filet: 70 pounds

Prawns: 150 pounds

Scallops: 80 pounds

Siam Cuisine features Bangkok home-style cooking. These are recipes that Somchai and Kwan have brought from Thailand and have shared with many happy and satisfied diners. This cookbook is the result of their desire to reach a larger audience. We have endeavored to make each recipe as correct as possible for the home kitchen. Not everyone wants twenty servings of Green Curry Pork for dinner, so these recipes have been reduced to typical family-sized servings. It was not just a matter of dividing the recipes in half or by twenty. Each recipe had to be made, tasted, adjusted, remade, and tasted again until the combinations of flavors and their intensities were correct.

In the process of testing the recipes in this book, I discovered that Thais, like various other ethnic groups, never measure anything when cooking at home. They can tell by the smell, color, taste, and texture of the food whether the proportions of the ingredients are correct, and they make the necessary adjustments by adding a pinch more of ground coriander or half a handful more of dried red chili peppers to give the dish the proper degree of hotness. It was therefore necessary to translate these pinches and handfuls into a standard form so that the recipes could be made in any American kitchen.

This took place either in the restaurant or their home. Somchai and Kwan had to measure the ingredients for each recipe, while I questioned them and took notes. At home I recreated the dish according to what I had seen and then took a sample back to them. They tasted it and recommended any necessary adjustments. I went back to my kitchen and made the recipe again, repeating the whole process until the flavors were just right. Testing all of the recipes in this book took me over three years—a time-consuming task but not a difficult one, since the recipes did after all originate in home kitchens.

For those readers who have not eaten at Siam Cuisine, I hope that you will try some of Somchai and Kwan's recipes and will enjoy them as much as my family and I have. For those who have eaten at Siam Cuisine, I would like to invite you to cook your favorite dishes at home, and also to try some of the recipes that do not appear on the menu.

Patricia Unterman, food critic for the San Francisco Chronicle, said it very well when she featured Siam Cuisine in her column shortly after the restaurant opened. On April 18, 1982, she wrote,

"Siam Cuisine in Berkeley is a marvelous restaurant. The food seems to cleanse and stimulate my overworked palate, and the wide range of dishes brings me back again and again. For food that is exciting, challenging and always delicious, Siam Cuisine is unique in the Bay Area."
© SAN FRANCISCO CHRONICLE, 1982
Reprinted by permission.

Diana Hiranaga

Putting Together a Thai Menu

For those of you who would like to create a Thai meal, we offer some thoughts, suggestions, and parameters to consider in choosing a menu. No matter what type of food is to be served, both the cook and the diner must be considered in designing the menu. The biggest obstacle to getting a meal on the table is selecting the entrees. If the entrees have been well chosen, everything else seems to fall into place.

Food must stimulate the nose and eyes as well as the palate by providing a variety of flavors, textures, and colors. When considering the menu, keep in mind what the physiologists tell us about the sense of taste. Our taste buds can distinguish only four basic flavors: sweet, sour, salty, and bitter. In the case of Thai food, however, we must defer to the Chinese who for centuries have also included "hot" on the list. A Thai meal will include all of these basic flavors, never overworking any one part of the palate.

In Thailand, food shopping is usually done twice a day. The variety of foods on the menu will depend on what is in season and available in the marketplace where the cook searches out the freshest foods for the day's meals.

A Thai meal never features a "main course." All the dishes are served together and eaten family-style, with each entree of equal importance. This will include chili peppers, lemon grass, galanga, lime leaf, basil, garlic, and shallots which Thai people consume in various combinations every day. Their meals will also frequently include fresh raw vegetables, dipped in acrid-smelling Shrimp Paste Sauce (page 93). Only one liquid dish will be offered; if hot and sour vegetable soup is served for dinner, curry will not be. There will be at least one spicy hot dish, with several others of varying intensities. These may include chicken, fish, and other meats. Salads are usually eaten as a snack or while enjoying an alcoholic beverage. If eaten for lunch or dinner, a salad is accompanied by rice, or will be added to the meal if another entree is needed.

6

The cook must employ a variety of cooking methods if all of the dishes are to reach the table at about the same time. One technique is to include recipes that can be prepared partially or totally in advance. Choose your menu so that you don't end up needing six burners when in fact you only have four. And don't attempt to prepare more than two stir-fry dishes, or the first ones will become cold before the last one has reached the table.

A good rule of thumb for the size of your Thai menu is to allow one dish per person, plus "one for the table." If unexpected guests drop in, instead of making additional entrees, just chop a little more of "this" meat and "that" vegetable to increase the volume of each dish. Just remember to adjust the seasoning!

The following five menus give an idea of what you might expect to be served at a typical family dinner in a Thai home. These menus are only suggestions for dishes that go well together; feel free to substitute your own favorites. Though not listed on the menus, rice is always included. Rice is the common denominator for all meals in Thailand and should be served with each meal.

Menu #1 (Serves 3)
Hot and Sour Prawn Soup
Sautéed Green Beans
Panang Beef
Ginger Chicken

Menu #2 (Serves 3)
Hot and Sour Vegetable Soup
Princess Favorite Pork
Chicken with Sweet Basil
Thai Egg Foo Yung

Menu #3 (Serves 3)
Fish Cakes
Broccoli Beef
Green Curry Pork
Prawns and Calamari with Spicy Chili Oil

Menu #4 (Serves 4)
Bitter Melon Soup with Spareribs
Deep-fried Fish with Red Curry Sauce
Sautéed Mixed Vegetable
Barbecued Chicken
Beef Salad I

Menu #5 (Serves 4)
Chinese Okra Soup
Salty Beef
Pork and Green Beans in Red Curry Paste
Prawns and Calamari with Sweet Basil
Braised Spareribs

The following three menus are examples of meals that Chai and Kwan have created for occasions that do not fall into the "typical family dinner" category. Again, these menus are only suggestions.

Gourmet Menu (Serves 4)
Thai Chicken Soup
Green Papaya Salad
Sautéed Green Beans
Steamed Fish Curry in Banana-Leaf Bowl
Rack of Lamb

Seafood Menu (Serves 5)
Prawn Salad
Prawns with Coconut-Flavored Rice Noodles
Fish in Tamarind Sauce
Pineapple Curry
Seafood Clay Pot
Calamari with Sweet Basil

Buffet Menu (Serves 8)
Thai Appetizers
Fresh Mixed Vegetables with Spicy Peanut Dressing
Beef Salad II
Thai Crisp-Fried Rice Threads
Shrimp and Ground Pork Toast
Yellow Curry Chicken
Barbecued Chicken
Thai Barbecued Spareribs

For those who would rather start on a smaller scale, serving only one or two Thai dishes, we offer the following list of some of the most popular dishes at Siam Cuisine.

The most frequently requested item on the menu is Beef Satay (page 41). Next come Phat Thai, or Thai Noodles, (page 158), Yellow Curry Chicken (page 116), Thai Chicken Soup (page 53), and Hot and Sour Prawn Soup (page 54). Other favorites are Panang Beef (page 106), Chicken with Sweet Basil (page 113), Fried Sweet Potato (page 43), Prawns and Calamari in Spicy Chili Oil (page 127), Fish Cakes (page 40), Ginger Chicken (page 117), Angel Wings (page 119), Prawns and Scallops with Sweet Basil (page 130), Lard Nar, or Broccoli over Fresh Rice Noodles, (page 160), and Ground Prawn Curry with Somen Noodles (page 165).

How To Use This Book

Cookbooks in Thailand are a recent innovation. Recipes have always been learned in the process of daily living. Exposure to food preparation starts in infancy, whether the family is growing food or shopping for it. For most young girls actual cooking begins in adolescence with the preparation of rice and slowly graduates into full participation with the other members of the the family.

Within the past ten years, though, this pattern has begun to change. With more people moving into the cities, with their abundance of prepared foods and restaurants, the people of Thailand are becoming somewhat removed from the traditional way of learning about food and its preparation. The result is a growing need for cookbooks.

Thai cooking is simple, based on common sense and experience. The season and the freshness of raw materials dictate what appears on the dinner table, and the palate of the cook determines the final flavoring. Even methods of preparing food are changing, depending on what utensils are available. There are many ways to crack a coconut; this book offers just one, which works well in Somchai and Kwan's kitchen. If you have a better method, please use it.

What this book offers are accurate measurements of raw ingredients and methods of cooking them so that the final product possesses the characteristic taste and texture of the food served at Siam Cuisine. In most cases we have given a standard measurement for each item listed in the recipe. For instance galanga, a ginger-like root, can now be purchased fresh or dried in cellophane packets in the San Francisco Bay Area. If only dried is available in your area, the size of each piece will vary. We have therefore offered a standard measurement that can be applied in the average kitchen.

We recommend following the recipes closely at first since many of the ingredients may be foreign and unfamiliar to you. With experience you will know what a particular spice does in various quantities and will be able to predict what the resulting taste will be. Once you have made a certain recipe a few times and become familiar with the ingredients, experiment by substituting or altering the quantity of the various ingredients according to your own taste, and adjusting the cooking time if necessary. It is in this spirit that we suggest you use this book, always using the freshest ingredients, your experience, and common sense to experiment with and adjust the recipes to suit your tastes and kitchen.

If time is limited, there are a few things that you can do to shorten your time in the kitchen. Some items do very well when prepared in bulk. Ingredients like ground peanuts, ground dried chili peppers, and minced garlic can be prepared ahead of time and stored until needed.

There are several sauces that are used repeatedly throughout this cookbook. At the restaurant the sauces are prepared in bulk and combined with the other ingredients only after a dish has been ordered. This works very well at the restaurant and can save a tremendous amount of time at home, as well, when you are trying to get a meal on the table. I always have a batch of Spicy Chili Oil (page 89) stored in the refrigerator. It is used in Peanut Curry Sauce (page 92), Musuman Curry (page 107), Prawns with Spicy Chili Oil (page 127), and Prawns and Calamari in Spicy Chili Oil (page 127). Basic Curry Paste (page 79) and Kwan's Sweet and Sour Sauce (page 87) are also good to keep on hand. Basic Curry Paste is used in Fish Cakes (page 40), Peanut Curry Sauce, Panang Beef (page 106), Red Curry Fish (page 144), and Fish Curry with Somen Noodles (page 162). Kwan's Sweet and Sour Sauce is used in many of the stir-fry dishes and as a base for several of the dipping sauces.

If properly stored, all of the curry pastes can be prepared in advance. It is often more practical to grind the pastes a day or two before they will be needed.

Another sauce you might want to have available is Spicy Chili Oil for Hot and Sour Prawn Soup (page 90), which is also added to the Seafood Clay Pot (page 151). The recipes for the Mee Krob (page 46) and Phat Thai sauces (page 158) can also be made in advance, and provide enough sauce for several dishes.

In many of the recipes several of the steps can be completed in advance, including those dishes like Angel Wings (page 119), Beef Satay (page 41), and Barbecued Chicken (page 122) that can be partially cooked the day before, then finished just before serving.

We recommend that you do all the cutting, chopping, and measuring of ingredients before the actual cooking starts, especially for stir-fried dishes. Timing is crucial with them, since the cooking proceeds quite rapidly. Read through the recipe and check the list of ingredients against those you have gathered. This way you won't burn the garlic or overcook the vegetables and meat because one item was overlooked and had to be chopped at the last minute.

Some of the recipe names, like "Peasant's Rice" and "Angel Wings," are not completely self-explanatory. Throughout the book we have used the names as they appear on the menu. For the non-customers we have included a description of each. A few of the recipes, such as those for charcoal-broiled fish, calamari, and scallops, are quite similar. We have included the full recipe for each version, to keep cross-referencing to a minimum.

If a recipe is designated "hot," it is hot. There are two with a "very hot" rating; they come with a warning. Reducing the amount of chili peppers will definitely lessen the intensity, but please do not elimi-nate them completely. They are vital to the finished dish, adding a piquant flavor and aroma.

The number of people the recipes will serve is given at the end of each one, and is based on a family-style dinner. "Serves 4" means that the recipe will feed four provided several other dishes are also included in the meal. Of course, this is only an approximation, and depends on the appetites of the diners.

In the cookbook we separate the recipes into categories based on the actual menu used in the restaurant. This is for easy referencing and is based on an American meal even though a Thai meal is eaten family-style.

We hope this book provides you with the necessary tools and guidance to create your own Thai cuisine, and we hope it will foster an enjoyment of the cooking adventure you are about to begin.

Typical Thai Kitchen Equipment

 In Thailand the best way to see how a Thai kitchen is equipped is to take a walking tour through a Bangkok marketplace. The sidewalk is lined on both sides with vendors hawking exuberant amounts of freshly prepared foods—snacks, salads, main courses, and desserts. A vendor carts his raw ingredients, stove, charcoal, wok, mortar and pestle, cleaver, cutting board, utensils, and low table and stool to his spot on the sidewalk, where he sits preparing his specialties until he is sold out. Then the shift changes and someone else comes in to occupy the spot, hauling in his own equipment. This activity goes on late into the night.

As you watch these vendors you begin to draw up a mental list of their equipment and ingredients and how each is used. Soon you recognize the basic simplicity behind all that activity.

The Thai kitchen is usually located outside, under a small over-hang. It is uncluttered and contains only a few basic tools and pieces of equipment. One of the most visible and important items in the kitchen is the charcoal stove, a freestanding structure formed from red clay. This funnel-shaped stove is vented through a low opening and the upper edge has several flanges to support a wok or pot. The charcoal is held in a clay vessel, which can be removed for cleaning.

An iron **wok** rests over the charcoal stove. The shape of a wok is very ingenious. The concave surface distributes the heat evenly and draws the food toward the center, allowing the cook to use smaller amounts of oil for stir-frying or deep-frying. The depth allows the cook to quickly stir and flip or toss the food. When you buy a new wok, scrub it with soap to remove the machine oil. Season the wok by placing it over low heat for several minutes. Add 1 to 2 tablespoons of cooking oil. Using a paper towel, evenly coat the entire inside surface of the wok, removing the excess. Continue to heat over low heat for 5 to 10 minutes. Repeat the process several times until the surface starts to darken. After season-ing, keep it clean by rinsing with hot water and scrubbing with a brush to remove any food particles. Then return it immediately to the fire to dry.

One of the most common tools in a Thai kitchen is the **mortar and pestle**. There are two basic types. The heavy stone mortar with a stone pestle is used to grind and crush everything from seeds to fish. They are usually handed down from generation to generation, the bowl getting deeper with prolonged use. The other type is made of clay with a wooden pestle. It has a deep cone-shaped bowl, which is advantageous for holding salads when combining and crushing the ingredients so that they will release their juices and absorb the flavors of the other ingredients, as in Green Papaya Salad (page 74).

Even though freshly shredded coconut can be purchased in the marketplace, many kitchens still display several utensils used in the preparation of coconut milk. A heavy, curved coconut knife is used to scrape the fiber from the coconut shell and to crack it in half. To remove the meat from the shell, a crescent-shaped metal blade with a serrated edge is attached to a small bench. The cook sits on the bench and scrapes the coconut halves against the blade. After processing, the coconut milk is strained through a tightly woven bamboo basket with two C-shaped handles, one on each side to rest over a bowl. (For instructions on preparing coconut milk, see page 22.)

In the past double-handled red **clay pots** with covers were a common item in Thailand. Curries, soups, and even rice were cooked in them over the charcoal stove. They can still be purchased in the marketplace, but have largely given way to the aluminum pot and the electric rice cooker in the kitchen. They are available in several sizes and shapes, and both the interior and exterior remain unglazed. When exposed to the direct heat of a charcoal stove, these pots may crack or break. If you cook with one of these Thai clay pots or a Chinese "sandy pot," completely submerge it in water for at least an hour each time before using it. When you remove the clay pot from the stove, do not place it on a cool surface, and do not place an empty one over a hot fire. If a clay pot is not available, a small metal one with a cover can be substituted.

This brief introduction has listed only the more basic items that are indispensable to a Thai kitchen. As you continue your walk through the market place, you will see chopping blocks made from cross-sections of trees, many types of knives and cleavers, and piles and piles of ceramic and metal pots and pans, pottery, steamers, plastic goods, baskets, dishes, glassware, brassware, and much, much more.

Ingredients

Many of the following ingredients can be found in Asian markets or in the Oriental food section of some supermarkets. There are others which I have only been able to find in markets specializing in products imported from Southeast Asia. I will specify in those cases where you can find them and also suggest other sources not listed above.

BAMBOO SHOOTS

The tender young shoots of the bamboo are available peeled and cooked. They are packed in cans and may be purchased whole, halved, sliced, or julienned. I have also found them freshly prepared in bulk in Asian and some produce markets.

BANANA BUDS

The actual bud is 10 to 13 inches long, tapering to a point. To use, discard the outer few petals. Remove the remaining petals, slice, and steam for about 15 minutes. The petals are very bitter, but steaming reduces the bitterness slightly. Beneath each of these reddish-purple petals are baby banana clusters which are also steamed and eaten in Thailand. Banana buds are often available in Southeast Asian Markets and occasionally in larger produce stores.

BANANA LEAVES

Banana plants are very common in Thailand, where the leaves are used to wrap food and to line steamers. They are also shaped into bowls for steaming desserts and fish curries. They can be purchased frozen at Southeast Asian markets. Defrost the leaves before using and wipe them with a damp cloth to remove any dirt. Pouring boiling water over them makes them pliable. If fresh leaves are available, we recommend using them, but the frozen ones do hold up very well.

BASIL

Six varieties of basil are commonly used for cooking in Thailand, of which three are used in this cookbook. Seeds and seedlings can be ordered or purchased from your nursery. (See Tomlinson's Nurseries on page 177.) The plants can also be propagated from cuttings.

Holy Basil

Holy basil is used in recipes that call for sweet basil. It has a delicate, slightly sweet clove flavor. It originated in India, and can be easily propagated from seed. The small, pointed, oval leaves have serrated edges. They are bright green, sometimes tinted purple. The stems and veins are hairy. Holy basil is usually cooked and is added to seafood or meat dishes at the last moment. At Siam Cuisine, orange mint (also known as orange bergamot mint), a member of the basil family, has been substituted because of its availability when the restaurant first opened. It has a shinier, rounder, purplish leaf with a citrus-like flavor.

Lemon Basil

This basil has a light, sweet, lemony flavor and aroma. The pale-green leaves are 2½ inches long by 1¼ inches wide, tapering to a point. In Thailand, it is added to salads or used to flavor soups. It can also be eaten raw as an accompaniment to Fish Curry with Somen Noodles (page 162).

Thai Basil

The leaves of Thai basil (also known as licorice basil) are 2 to 3 inches in length and half as wide. They are shiny green in color, with purple veining. The oil of this basil has a strong anise smell and flavor. Add it at the last moment to salads, curries, seafood, and sautéed chicken dishes. Thai basil can now be found year-round in the San Francisco Bay Area at Southeast Asian markets and at large produce stores. If unavailable, substitute Italian sweet basil. Thai basil will last 7 to 10 days in the refrigerator; keep the stems in water, changing periodically, and cover the leaves loosely with a plastic bag.

BEAN SAUCE, BROWN

Brown bean sauce consists of fermented soybeans with salt, flour, and water. Its color varies from light brown to dark brown, and it is available with whole beans or ground beans. It adds a salty, full-bodied flavor as well as texture to many dishes. Once opened, store it in the refrigerator in a tightly sealed jar. It will keep indefinitely.

BEAN SAUCE, YELLOW

The yellow bean sauce recommended for use in these recipes is a Thai brand whose label reads "yellow bean sauce" in English and "white bean sauce" in Thai. It comes in a 16-ounce, short, wide jar. The beans are whole and yellowish white in color. The other type, which is not recommended, is very salty and comes in a tall, thin jar whose label reads "yellow bean sauce" in Thai, so check the label carefully.

BEAN SPROUTS

The young, tender sprouts of the mung bean are about 2½ inches long. They add a crisp texture to salads and noodle dishes. If they are not available fresh, sprout them as you would alfalfa sprouts. Keep them in the refrigerator for up to one week in a sealed plastic bag.

BITTER MELON

This relative to the cucumber is 5 to 10 inches long and 2 to 2½ inches in diameter, with one end tapering to a point. The surface of the light green melon is covered with fissures running down its length. Before using, scrape out the pith and the seeds with a spoon. This melon is very bitter, but when blanched or cooked in soups, its bitterness is diluted.

BLACK BEANS, DRIED

In Thailand, black beans are used mainly for desserts. Soak them in water overnight before using.

BLUE LAKE GREEN BEAN

Similar to the Kentucky Wonder green beans, Blue Lake green beans are smaller, rounder, and stringless. Other types of green beans can be substituted if these are unavailable.

BRINE-CURED RADISH

After curing in salt, these long white radishes become dark brown, slightly shiny, and sticky, with an almost leathery quality. However, they are still crunchy, with a salty and slightly sweet flavor. They are usually packaged in 16-ounce cellophane bags. Stored in the refrigerator in a sealed plastic bag, they will last indefinitely. Rinse before using.

CABBAGE, PRESERVED

Preserved cabbage, also called Tianjin Preserved Vegetables and *Dung Choy*, is sold in round, squat, glass or clay crocks. The cabbage has been coarsely chopped and flavored with garlic, salt, and sometimes sugar. The pieces are relatively dry, and are light brown in color. In Thailand, preserved cabbage is used mainly in noodle soup.

CALAMARI

The calamari, or squid, used in the restaurant comes seven to twelve pieces per pound. Most calamari has been frozen, although it can be purchased fresh in season. At the restaurant, the cooks parboil the calamari for a few seconds just before combining it with the other ingredients. This ensures they aren't overcooked, and each piece stays tender.

To clean calamari

Pull the head away from the body section, removing the entrails and the transparent cartilage or quill in the process. Under slowly running water remove the skin from the body and rinse out any organs remaining in the cavity. Cut the body lengthwise or in rings as required by the recipe.

Cut the head section between the eyes and tentacles. Discard the eyes and attached entrails. Check to be sure that the beak has been discarded with the eyes. Trim away the tops of the tentacles, if you like, to give them a uniform look when cooked.

CARDAMOM SEEDS AND PODS

These seeds are collected from the pods of plants belonging to the ginger family. The beige pods are about ½ inch long and contain about 10 to 17 grey-brown seeds that have a mentholated, ginger-licorice flavor. Grind the seeds in a mortar just before using, since much of the flavor is lost when the spice is stored in powdered form.

CHICKEN

The chickens available in the United States are different from those in Thailand. Kwan calls them "business chickens," as opposed to the homegrown type. In Thailand, chickens are allowed to run around and forage. After being slaughtered, they are hung up to dry while waiting to be sold in the marketplace. In the United States, chickens contain a lot of water from processing. The meat and bones are soft and cannot be stewed like those in Thailand.

In Thailand, chicken curries are stewed with the bones intact. Somchai and Kwan have tried it here, but with little success—the meat turns to mush and disintegrates. Therefore at the restaurant they have adjusted their recipes to accommodate the local product. The chickens are boned and chicken stock is added to give the curry the flavor and sweetness of the bones.

To bone a chicken

Cut the skin lengthwise down the center back of the chicken. Slice the meat from either side of the breastbone down the full length of the chicken.

To remove the chicken wings, pull the skin away from the joint. Hold a wing in one hand and cut through the joint without cutting the skin, severing all the tendons. Pull the wing toward the tail until all the skin, with breast meat attached, is removed from the carcass. Pull the breast meat from the skin and cut at the joint. Do not cut the skin. Set aside. Repeat for the other wing. The chicken wings, with all the skin intact, are ready to be used in Angel Wings (page 119). Remove the excess skin if preparing any of the other recipes requiring chicken wings.

Remove the breast filet from the carcass and set aside. Disjoint the legs, separating the thighs and drumsticks. Make a cut down the length of each leg section to the bone. Remove the meat by cutting around the bone. Use the meat in various chicken dishes, and store the bones in the freezer until you have accumulated enough to make Chicken Stock (page 53).

CHILI PEPPERS

Chili peppers are the little capsicums that add the heat to Thai food. They are rich in minerals and vitamins, especially C and A, and are said to aid digestion as well as stimulate the appetite. Some people go so far as to say they are addictive. They have even been called the aphrodisiac of the eighties. First imported to Thailand over 400 years ago, this domesticated weed is the New World's contribution to Thai cuisine.

Because of the ease with which they hybridize, there are many varieties of the chili pepper. Immature chili peppers are commonly eaten fresh, while the mature red ones are usually dried. Fresh chilies come in many sizes, in a spectrum of colors from green to yellow to red, and in degrees of hotness from mild to incendiary. In general, the smaller the chili, the hotter it is. You may adjust the amount or size of chili peppers in each recipe according to your taste, but always add some for the sweet, fresh perfume and flavor they impart. After working with the various types of chili peppers, you will become more familiar with them and will be able to adjust the hotness to your own liking. Handle the chili peppers, fresh or dried, with care, remembering that most of the heat is concentrated in the veins and seeds. Wash your hands thoroughly after cutting or chopping peppers to remove the oils, and take care not to rub your eyes or nose after handling them!

Cayenne Peppers, Dried

Cayenne peppers are 2 to 4 inches long and ⅜ inch in diameter and are very hot. They can be purchased whole, ground, or in flakes. You can make your own flakes by dry-roasting whole dried cayenne peppers in a clean skillet until they turn a deep, dark red. Then pound them into small flakes using a mortar. Store in a tightly sealed jar.

Dried Red Chilies

Dried red chili peppers, usually 2 to 3 inches long and ½ inch wide, are imported from Thailand and sold in Southeast Asian markets for use in curries and other dishes. They are very aromatic and very hot. Choose dried chili peppers that are dark red, since the intensity of color seems to be proportional to the intensity of flavor. If they are not available, use cayenne peppers, which are slightly hotter. For curry pastes, soak them in water until soft, remove the seeds, and pound.

Jalapeño chilies

Jalapeños are dark green and very hot. They are about 2½ inches long and 1 inch wide at the stem, tapering to a blunt point. This is the fresh chili used at Siam Cuisine. Serrano chilies can be substituted for jalapeños.

New Mexico or California Chilies, Dried

The New Mexico and California chili peppers are very similar in appearance. Both are deep, dark red and are about 5 to 6 inches long and 2 to 2½ inches wide. Used interchangeably, they add little or no hotness but do add a rich flavor. They are sometimes roasted before using to enhance their flavor. Several of the curry paste recipes call for this type of chili. They are basically added for color to make the finished curry "look pretty."

Serrano Chilies

Serrano chili peppers look very similar to jalapeños but are darker green and don't taper as much. They are about 1½ inches long and ¾ inch wide. They can be used interchangeably with jalapeños.

Thai Chilies (Phik Kii Nu)

These tiny chili peppers are extremely hot. They are 1½ to 2 inches long and ¼ inch in diameter. These small, thin peppers are very aromatic with a rich, full flavor and can be purchased fresh at Southeast Asian markets. Store them in the refrigerator, wrapped in a paper towel and sealed in a plastic bag. Any small, fresh chili can be substituted.

CHILI SAUCE, RED

There are several types and brands of red chili sauce. They all contain coarsely ground red chilies in various combinations with oil, salt, vinegar, sugar, and garlic. They have a lumpy texture and brownish-red color. They vary in hotness so find one you like and use it according to your taste in the dipping sauce recipes. Once the jar is opened, store it in the refrigerator.

CHILI SAUCE, SRIRACHA

This sauce was originally made in the town of Sriracha, Thailand. It is a mixture of finely ground and seeded red chili peppers, vinegar, sugar, garlic, and water. This bright orange sauce has a tangy, piercing, sweet and sour flavor that comes mild, medium, and hot. It is used as a dipping sauce for seafood, and in several of the salads in this cookbook. Once opened, store it in the refrigerator.

CHINESE CELERY

Chinese celery looks and grows very much like Italian parsley. It is greener than celery but lighter than Italian parsley. The flavor is very much like celery but slightly stronger. In Thailand it is generally used to flavor soups. If it is not available, the center stalks of young celery make a good substitute.

CINNAMON

Native to South Asia, cinnamon is the dried inner bark of the branches of a tree from the laurel family. It is rarely used in Thai cooking except in those dishes that show an Indian influence, such as Peanut Curry Sauce (page 92) and Musuman Curry (page 107).

CLOVES

The dried flower buds of a tropical myrtle tree, cloves are used in Thai dishes that show an Indian influence. For the best flavor, buy whole cloves and grind your own.

COCONUT MILK

Most of the recipes in this cookbook that use coconut milk call for "thick" coconut milk—the liquid from the first pressing of fresh coconut meat that has been ground with water. "Thin" coconut milk is the liquid from successive pressings. Our recipe for thick coconut milk combines the liquid from the first and second pressing.

If fresh coconuts are not available, frozen, shredded coconut may be used. However, in our experience, the quality of frozen shredded coconut is not high, and it makes a very thin milk. Shredded, unsweetened, desiccated coconut may be used, but we feel if freshly shredded coconut is not available, canned is the best substitute. In fact, even the quality of homemade coconut milk can vary tremendously in this country depending on the freshness of the coconut used. We, therefore, recommend making fresh coconut milk for use only in desserts for that "fresh coconut" smell. For most of the recipes in this cookbook we recommend canned or frozen coconut milk, for both its quality and its convenience.

When using canned coconut milk, shake it thoroughly before using to combine the liquid with the separated "cream." If a recipe specifies coconut cream, do not shake the can, and refrigerate for several hours before opening. Scoop out and reserve the separated solids. Using a fine strainer, strain and discard the liquid, saving any remaining "cream."

A number of brands of canned coconut milk are available. Try a different kind each time you make a curry until you find the one that you like best. Look for a brand that releases the coconut oil most quickly when reduced in preparing a curry.

If you do decide to make your own coconut milk for use in one of the curry recipes, eliminate the water that the meat is cooked in, and cook the meat directly in the curry.

To make thick coconut milk from fresh coconuts (maphrao):

To make your own thick coconut milk, start with fresh, mature coconuts. Choose coconuts that look fresh, are heavy for their size, and still have liquid inside. If the coconut has an odor when cracked, don't use it.

Soak the whole coconut in water for about 1 minute so that it won't shatter when cracked. Use a large cleaver to cut away the loose fibers on the outside of the shell so they won't contaminate the meat. Place the coconut on a solid surface, and use the back edge of a cleaver to strike the coconut just once very hard across the grain.

This will put one crack around the circumference of the coconut. Work the sharp edge of the cleaver into the crack and separate the two halves. The liquid inside the coconut is not used to make coconut milk; however, it makes a refreshing drink.

Use a heavy tablespoon to scrape the meat from inside the two coconut halves. Start at the upper edge, scraping around the top, and work toward the center. (In Thailand, a crescent-shaped metal coconut scraper is used to scrape the meat from the shell—see page 14.) If you are making coconut milk for desserts, cut away and discard all of the dark inner skin, which tends to discolor the milk. For use in curries, however, small pieces of the inner skin will not affect the results.

The shredded coconut can be stored in the refrigerator for 2 to 3 days, or frozen for later use. One medium coconut will make enough coconut milk for any of the curry recipes in this book. (In Thailand, finely shredded fresh coconut can be purchased in bulk.)

Ingredients for coconut milk:

Shredded meat from 1 medium fresh coconut (approximately 3 cups, packed)
3½ cups hot water

Combine half of the shredded coconut and 1½ cups hot water in a blender. Grind until liquefied. (Grinding the coconut in two batches will keep your blender from overheating.) Pour the contents of the blender into a large bowl and knead with your hands. Pour through a large, fine strainer into another bowl. With your hands, squeeze the coconut meat to extract any remaining milk.

Set the used coconut meat aside and pour the coconut milk back into the blender. Add the rest of the shredded coconut and 1½ cups hot water to the blender. Grind until liquefied and extract the coconut milk as above. Set the coconut milk aside.

Combine the two batches of used coconut meat and add the remaining ½ cup hot water. Knead with your hands. Strain again, squeezing the coconut meat with your hands to extract all of the milk. Discard the used coconut meat. (In Thailand, it would be fed to the chickens.)

Coconut milk can be stored in the refrigerator for 2 to 3 days or in the freezer for future use, if properly sealed.

Makes approximately 3½ cups.

CORIANDER, FRESH (LEAVES, SEEDS, AND ROOTS)

Thais use all parts of the coriander plant. The leaves, which have a musky flavor, are added to sauces and curries and are used as a garnish. The roots and seeds are pounded into curry pastes. Dry-roasting the seeds before pounding heightens their flavor.

The word coriander often refers to the seeds only, while cilantro or Chinese parsley refers to the fresh leaves and roots. In this cookbook, however, we use "coriander" for all forms, and specify in each recipe whether seeds, leaves, or roots are needed.

Store fresh coriander in the refrigerator for up to a week with the roots in water and the leaves covered with a plastic bag; or wrap it in a damp paper towel inside a plastic bag and keep refrigerated. In Thailand, coriander is sold with the long roots intact. The roots of the fresh coriander sold here are usually trimmed to a stub or completely removed. When roots are available, freeze them for future use. The seeds will keep indefinitely. Coriander can easily be grown from seeds.

CORN, BABY

Canned baby corn is available in Asian markets and in specialty/ gourmet shops. If fresh is available, we recommend using it because the taste is superior. Husk as you would mature corn, and use like the canned variety. Eat the whole corn, cob and all.

CORNSTARCH

Combined with water, cornstarch is used as a tasteless thickening agent in stir-fry dishes. When cooked, it becomes clear. To avoid lumps, stir the cornstarch and water thoroughly just before adding to the dish.

CUMIN

Common to Mexican, Latin American, Creole, North African, Middle Eastern, Indian, and Southeast Asian cuisines, cumin is a member of the Umbelliferae family. It is available as whole seeds or ground into a fine powder. In Thailand, when the seeds are used in curry pastes, they are roasted and ground in a mortar, exuding a fuller flavor.

CURRY PASTE

Curry paste in Thailand is a pungent blend of herbs and spices that have been ground into a fine paste—quite different from the familiar British version of "curry powder". The color of the curry paste is determined by the type of chili used. The red curry pastes use red chilies and the green curry pastes use green Thai chilies and fresh coriander; both pastes are hot. Yellow curry paste is colored by curry powder and is of Muslim origin.

The best curry pastes are ground in a mortar to bring out the juices and blend the flavors. (Of course, you can also use an electric spice grinder and/or a blender.) The Thai method of determining if the proportions are correct is to look at the paste and taste it. If necessary, more ingredients may be added. The dry spices for the curry paste are roasted in an ungreased pan over medium-high heat until browned to heighten their smell and taste.

To make the curry paste in a mortar, pound the ingredients in the following order: roasted seeds, Kaffir lime rind, galanga, lemon grass, shallots, dried chili peppers, and garlic. Salt is added, as needed, ½ teaspoon at a time to accelerate the process and to hold the ingredients together while pounding. If the paste gets too wet, squeeze out the liquid, reserve, and add to the paste when pounding is completed. If the mortar becomes full, remove some of the paste and continue with the next ingredient, combining all the ingredients at the end. Be sure to pound or grind thoroughly; any large pieces will taste bitter.

Curry pastes can be stored for up to 3 weeks in the refrigerator or 3 months in the freezer.

Curries are the main food of Thais in the cities. Southern Thai curries use coconut milk, which is also common in the curries of southern India. The curries of Northern Thailand are made without coconut milk, giving them a different texture and quality.

FISH, GROUND

Ground fish is available in Asian fish markets. It should be light in color and clear, almost transparent. Avoid ground fish that has a red tint from too much salt or appears white from too much flour. Before using, taste for salt content and, if necessary, adjust the amount of salt or fish sauce in the recipe. If ground fish is not available in your area, you can make your own by grinding to a fine paste 1 pound of any firm-fleshed, white fish filet in a food processor. In a bowl combine the ground fish, 2 egg whites, 2 tablespoons flour, and 1¼ teaspoon salt. The mixture is now ready to be used in Fish Cakes (page 40). However, the texture will be different from that of the commercially prepared ground fish.

FISH SAUCE (NAM PLA)

Fish sauce is the liquid extracted from salted, fermented anchovies. This clear, reddish-brown liquid with its strong fishy odor is used to flavor and salt foods in much the same way as soy sauce is used in China and Japan. Try several brands to find one that you like, since they do vary in saltiness.

FUNGUS, BLACK (CLOUD EARS)

Two varieties of black fungus are commonly available in Asian markets. The larger, thicker variety is called *wood ears*, and the smaller type is called *cloud ears*. The recipes in this cookbook call for cloud ears, which have a more delicate consistency. This fungus grows on trees and is sold in cellophane packages in dried form, looking somewhat like small charcoal shavings. Before using, rehydrate them in water for about 5–10 minutes. They will expand into gelatinous, yet crunchy morsels that have little flavor of their own. Stored in dried form, they will last indefinitely.

GALANGA

Galanga or greater galangal, also called *kha* in Thailand, *laos* in Vietnam and Indonesia, and Siamese ginger, is a member of the ginger family that is very common in Southeast Asia, where it is used for medicinal as well as culinary purposes. This rhizome can be found in fresh, frozen, dried, and powdered forms in Southeast Asian markets and fresh in some large produce markets. The subterranean stem looks similar to ginger but grows with all of its new shoots pointing up from its round main stem, which is 1 to 2 inches in diameter with light tan skin and darker tan stripes. It has been described as tasting like paint thinner smells and is used to flavor soups and curries.

Fresh and frozen galanga are interchangeable. Defrost the frozen type before using, cutting away any soggy parts. Peeling is optional. Always use fresh when available, but dried galanga can be substituted by decreasing the amount by a third. Dried galanga comes in pieces of various sizes, which can be stored indefinitely in a sealed jar. Don't use powdered galanga; the smell and taste are greatly reduced.

In soups be careful not to overcook fresh galanga or its flavor and fragrance will be dissipated. Thinly sliced fresh galanga added to soups can be eaten, but don't eat the dried type. For use in curry paste, slice the galanga as thin as possible to break down the fibers. There is no substitute for galanga.

GARLIC, FRESH

Garlic is used so extensively in Thai cooking that it is not unusual to see bunches of it hanging in the kitchen, waiting to be consumed. It is used throughout the cuisine, from curries to "cookies" (page 174).

There are basically two types of garlic in Thailand. The most common is similar to the type found in this country, but smaller, with numerous cloves per head. It has a very thin inner skin that does not have to be peeled and can be pounded directly into the curry pastes. The other type consists of a single bulb, resembling a pearl onion in size and shape, identical in taste to the multi-cloved variety.

Before mincing or chopping garlic, smash the cloves with the side of a cleaver to release more of the flavor. If you happen to burn the garlic while sautéing, discard it and start over, because the bitter flavor of burned garlic will alter the flavor of the final product.

You can store whole heads for up to a month in a dark, cool, well-ventilated area. Chopped or minced garlic, completely covered with oil, can be kept in the refrigerator in a tightly sealed jar for 4 to 5 weeks or can be frozen.

GARLIC, PICKLED AND PRESERVED

Pickled garlic and preserved garlic are very similar in appearance and taste. They are sold in jars by name and have been preserved in vinegar, sugar, and salt in different combinations. As we use the terms, pickled garlic means a brand that has a tart, garlicky flavor, while preserved garlic means a brand whose flavor is basically sweet. Interchanging the two will alter the flavor of the completed recipe slightly.

GINGER

Ginger is a rhizome with a pale yellowish-tan skin, which should be peeled before using. Always use fresh ginger, choosing only the firmest pieces. Ginger has a very pungent flavor; when used in large quantities, it can add considerable heat to a dish.

GOLDEN MOUNTAIN SAUCE

Golden Mountain is the brand name of a soy bean sauce. It looks very similar to soy sauce, but has a distinctive flavor and is used mainly for cooking rather than as a table sauce. It can be purchased in bottles at Southeast Asian markets.

HOISIN SAUCE

This thick, smooth, dark reddish-brown sauce has a sweet, tangy, spicy flavor that goes well with seafood, pork, and duck. It is made with soybeans, vinegar, sugar, salt, garlic, chilies, and spices and is available in cans and jars. Stored in a tightly sealed jar in the refrigerator, it will keep almost indefinitely.

KAFFIR LIME, RIND AND JUICE

The Kaffir lime tree or *makrut* is a member of the citrus family, with fruit the size of a regular lime. (See Tomlinson's Nurseries on page 177.) This lime has a very dark green, bumpy rind that is rich in oils, giving it a very sweet, citrus-like fragrance. Small dried slices are available packaged in cellophane at Southeast Asian markets. To use, soak slices in hot water for 1 to 2 hours until soft. Scrape off the white pith before cutting and measuring. Stored in a sealed jar, the dried pieces will keep indefinitely. Substitute the zest of regular lime if Kaffir lime is not available.

The juice of the Kaffir lime is used in Ground Prawn Curry with Somen Noodles (page 165) and adds a sweet aromatic flavor. If unavailable, regular lime juice may be substituted.

KAFFIR LIME LEAF

The leaves of the Kaffir lime tree are double, growing end to end, from 3 to 4½ inches in total length. When a recipe in this cookbook calls for one leaf, it refers to both sections. They are used whole or finely slivered to flavor soups, fish cakes, and sauces, and as a garnish. If fresh or frozen Kaffir lime leaves are not available, substitute fresh lime leaves or dried Kaffir lime leaves. Soak the dried leaves in water for about half an hour before using. Freshly frozen or dried leaves can be purchased in Southeast Asian markets. The leaves are also available in powdered form, but their taste and texture are inferior.

KRACHAI

Krachai, also known as "lesser ginger" and "rhizome," is grown in Southern China, where it is used for medicinal purposes. In Thailand this relative of ginger is added to curries, giving them a very distinctive smell and flavor. The rhizome has a light brown skin and a yellowish interior. It consists of many thin, fleshy fingers extending downward from the main stem. It is available in whole, sliced, and powdered forms in Southeast Asian markets. Whole *krachai* is available frozen, while the sliced is either dried or preserved in jars. The frozen and preserved varieties work best in these recipes.

LEMON GRASS

Lemon grass bestows a delicate lemony flavor and aroma on many Thai soups, salads, and curries. This sedge, a grass-like plant which resembles a green onion, has a long, pale green bulb about 13 to 14 inches, composed of fibrous sheathing layers. For use in curries and salads, thinly slice the stalk, discarding the upper quarter if it appears dry. Dried sliced lemon grass is also available; it can be reconstituted in hot water and used in the same amounts as fresh. You can also grow your own by rooting a stalk in 2 inches of water. Change the water every 3 or 4 days and plant the stalk in soil shortly after the roots appear.

LETTUCE, SALTED

Salted lettuce is sold in 5-ounce cans. The ingredients listed on the label are lettuce, salt, and water; however, it does have a slightly sweet taste. The lettuce is sliced into large pieces and canned in its brine. In Thailand it is made into a salad and eaten as a snack with rice. You can purchase it in Thai and Southeast Asian markets.

LIME

Thai limes are small, very juicy, and stronger in flavor than those found here. They are used in dipping sauces, soups, salads, and marinades, and as a garnish. We recommend using only fresh lime juice in the recipes; don't use the bottled type.

LIMESTONE PASTE

This finely ground pinkish-red mineral paste comes in a small round plastic container. It is used in desserts and in deep-frying batter for crisper results. It is sometimes made into a liquid, but for Fried Sweet Potato (page 43) it is used in paste form. Store it in an airtight jar once the plastic container has been opened. Purchase it in Southeast Asian markets.

MINT LEAVES

Most of the many varieties of mint will do well in the recipes. Since it is readily available in the supermarkets and produce markets, and is very easy to grow, we recommend using only fresh mint in these recipes.

MUNG BEANS, DRIED, PEELED, AND SPLIT

Dried mung beans are available in two forms. The most common type, from which bean sprouts are grown, has the outer green skin intact. The other type has been peeled, exposing the yellow bean, and is usually split. They are available in bulk or in cellophane packages at Asian markets, health food stores, and East Indian markets. For the recipes in this book use the peeled, split type.

MUSHROOMS, BLACK

Usually sold in dried form, the caps of these mushrooms have an uneven surface and come in a variety of shades from brown to black. They vary in quality, which determines the price; they tend to be expensive. To use, soak them in hot water for about 20 minutes until tender; drain; remove and discard the stems. Stored in an airtight jar, they will last indefinitely. In this cookbook they are used in soups, but they can also be added to stir-fried and braised dishes.

MUSSELS

Live mussels can be purchased from fish stores or from the meat section of some supermarkets. They begin to decompose rapidly once they die, so cook this shellfish while still alive. Discard any that remain open after handling and those whose shells can be easily twisted along their adjoining edges. To clean them, pull or cut off the "beard," scrub the outside of the shell with a vegetable brush, and rinse. Cook them for 3 to 5 minutes, until they open and the meat pulls away slightly from the shell. Don't overcook them, or they will shrink and become tough. Discard any that remain closed after cooking.

NAPA CABBAGE

Napa, or *nappa*, cabbage is a compact head of long, broad, pale green leaves that are slightly ruffled at the ends. The smooth base of the leaves is almost translucent. This mild-flavored cabbage is now available year-round. It can be stir-fried, and is used in soups and stews.

NOODLES

Noodles are second to rice in importance in a Thai meal. Like rice they can be eaten at all three meals and sometimes in between. Cooked in soup, sautéed, or fried, noodles come in different sizes and are made from different types of flour.

Fresh Egg Noodles

Fresh egg noodles are available fresh or frozen at Asian markets. They are made from wheat flour, water, and eggs and have a light yellow-tan tint. They come in several thicknesses, but for our purposes the "regular" thickness is best. Deep-fry them in Noodle Delight (page 161).

Fresh Rice Noodles

Fresh rice noodles consist of rice flour and water steamed in layers. They are sold in Chinatown in sheets about 1/16 inch thick which have been sliced into strips 3/8 inch wide and packaged in cellophane. The freshest noodles are tender to the touch; they become firmer and more difficult to separate the longer they sit. Use them for Lard Nar (page 160).

Jantaboon Rice Sticks

Jantaboon rice sticks are traditionally used in Thailand to make Phat Thai (page 158). They are made in the city of Jantaboon—the only town in Thailand that makes them. These white, translucent noodles are about 3/32 inch wide and 1/32 inch thick, and are also used in noodle soups. They must be soaked in cold water for 15 minutes before use or they will be crumbly when cooked.

Mung Bean Thread

Mung bean threads, also called cellophane noodles and *saifun*, are similar to rice threads or rice sticks but are made from mung bean starch/flour. When reconstituted, these thin, clear noodles are used in Angel Wings (page 119) and Bean Thread Salad (page 71).

Rice Thread or Sticks

Rice threads are dried, round noodles made with ground rice and water. They are small in diameter, clear, and very brittle, much like mung bean thread and are used in Mee Krob (page 46) and Mee Siam (page 163). Before they are incorporated into Mee Krob, the dried noodles are deep-fried into crisp, puffy strands.

Somen

Somen are thin, fragile, white noodles made from hard-wheat flour. Also called Japanese vermicelli, they come in 8- to 14-ounce packages.

OIL

Most cooking oils, like peanut or vegetable, can be used in the recipes. They have a high burning temperature, which is recommended for use in stir-fry dishes.

OKRA, CHINESE

Actually an elongated squash about 10 to 12 inches long with ridges running down its length, this vegetable looks like a large okra. Also known as luffa acutangula, it has a sweet, delicate flavor.

Before cooking, remove the ridges with a vegetable peeler. It is available in season in Asian markets and some large produce markets.

OYSTER SAUCE

Oyster sauce is a thick, dark brown sauce sold in bottles or large rectangular cans in bulk. It is made from oysters, salt, water, and cornstarch and is sometimes called oyster-flavored sauce. Oyster sauce without cornstarch as a thickener is also available, but is very expensive.

PALM SUGAR (COCONUT SUGAR)

Palm or coconut sugar is very similar in taste to maple sugar. In Thai cooking it is often added when sautéing dried red chili peppers to heighten the red color. The sap from palm trees is tapped and boiled down until crystallized into a thick, sticky, light-brown sugar. It is available in cans or jars. Once opened, store the unused portion in a tightly sealed jar. It does not need to be refrigerated and will keep indefinitely. A good substitute is obtained by mixing equal parts of brown sugar and molasses.

PAPAYA, GREEN

In Thailand many varieties of papaya, some as long as 10 inches, are available in the marketplaces. The unripe or green papaya is used as a vegetable in curries without coconut milk and in Green Papaya Salad (page 74). Recently, they have been showing up in Southeast Asian markets in the San Francisco Bay Area. Also check at your local specialty produce markets.

PEANUTS

These underground legumes are high in protein and rich in vitamins A and B. The recipes require raw peanuts that have been shelled and blanched to remove the inner, reddish-brown skin. To maximize their flavor, dry-roast and grind the raw peanuts each time they are needed. However, for convenience they can be roasted and ground in bulk. Stored in a tightly sealed jar, the ground peanuts will keep 4 to 5 months. Shelled, unsalted, roasted peanuts may also be ground as a substitute.

To dry-roast raw peanuts, place about 1 cup in a clean, dry wok over low to medium-low heat. Flip the peanuts constantly for about 20 minutes, until they are golden brown. Be careful not to let them burn. Remove from heat and allow to cool. At this point they can either be stored whole or ground in a mortar or blender. Grind a handful at a time until they are the size of large grains of sand. If you use a blender, the grinding will take just a few seconds. Don't grind them too fine or they will turn into peanut butter. Store in a tightly sealed jar.

PEPPERCORN, BLACK

Black peppercorns are whole, unripened pepper berries, that have been fermented and dried. Before the chili pepper was introduced from the New World around the sixteenth century, black pepper added the "hotness" to Thai cooking. Always use whole peppercorns and grind your own; pre-ground pepper quickly loses its flavor.

PEPPERCORNS, WHITE

White peppercorn is the seed of the ripe pepper berry. Grown on a tropical vine, the berries are soaked in water until the fruit falls away from the seed. Lime may be added to bleach the seeds.

PRAWNS

When medium prawns, or shrimp, are indicated in this cookbook, we mean 26 to 30 pieces per pound. At some fish markets these are called large prawns. To keep from overcooking the prawns at Siam Cuisine, they are parboiled for just a few seconds and then added to the dish at the last minute for the final cooking.

RADISH, SALTED

In Thailand, salted radish is sautéed with eggs and usually eaten at breakfast. The radish is shredded and preserved in salt and brown sugar, giving it a light brown color. It is sold in 8-ounce cellophane packages at Southeast Asian markets.

RICE

In Thailand rice is served with every meal and is consumed in copious amounts. The importance of rice, or *kow*, is reflected in the Thai language. *Kin*, which means "to eat," is combined with *kow*; *kin kow* means "let's eat," regardless of what is actually eaten.

Forty or fifty years ago rice was cooked over a charcoal stove in a clay pot. In the hands of an experienced cook, it would come out perfect every time. Mastering this technique was often frustrating and costly since the clay pots were fragile and would break if not properly tended. These days, however, aluminum pots and the Japanese electric rice cooker mean that even the novice can cook perfect rice.

Long-grain nonglutinous rice is a staple item in central and southern Thailand. Various types of nonglutinous rice are available in Thailand, but the Thais love jasmine rice. It is long grain, and when steamed, has a hint of jasmine aroma and flavor.

In northern Thailand, glutinous or sweet rice is served with the meal. It is called "sticky rice," and is eaten with the hands. This variety is also long grain and is used throughout the country for desserts. The sweet rice available in the United States is from Japan, and has a shorter, rounder grain.

To make rice

> 2 cups jasmine rice
> Water

Rinse the rice several times, until the water runs clear. Add water to cover so that the water level is 1 inch above the rice. Cover and bring to a boil over high heat. Mix with chopsticks or a fork to prevent the rice from sticking to the bottom, removing any grains that may have already stuck. Tightly cover and simmer over low heat for about 20 minutes, until the water has been absorbed. Turn off the heat and let sit for about 10 minutes.

Before serving, gently mix the rice to fluff it up.

Serves 4.

RICE FLOUR

Rice flour is ground from long-grain rice into a fine, silky powder. Purchase it in 1-pound plastic bags.

RICE FLOUR, SWEET

Sweet rice flour, also called glutinous rice flour, is ground from raw glutinous rice. It is used to make sweets and desserts, giving them a sticky, chewy quality. It is sold in 1-pound plastic bags.

SARDINES IN TOMATO SAUCE

The sardines come in 3.75 and 15-ounce cans and are very inexpensive. Kwan's mother created a salad with these that has become a family favorite (page 70).

SESAME OIL

Sesame oil is treasured throughout Asia for its nutty flavor and aroma. This dark amber oil, which is extracted from roasted sesame seeds, is rarely used for cooking because of its strong flavor and low burning temperature. Instead, it is added to dishes at the last moment.

SHALLOTS

The shallots available in Thailand are slightly smaller and stronger in flavor than those found here. It is not unusual to find bunches of shallots and garlic hanging in a Thai kitchen; both are used extensively in their cooking. If shallots are not available, substitute yellow onions.

SHRIMP, DRIED

Dried shrimp have a salty flavor and come in several sizes. We suggest using the larger ones in the recipes because they have better flavor; but if they are not available, the smaller ones will do just fine. Choose shrimp that have a light pinkish-orange color. The duller and darker the color, the older the shrimp. They are packaged by various weights in cellophane bags.

To make ground dried shrimp, place the dried shrimp in a blender and grind until all the pieces have turned to powder.

SHRIMP PASTE

Unlike the Chinese version of shrimp paste, which is pinkish-grey and runny, Thai shrimp paste is dark brown and very dry. It is made by alternately pounding and drying decomposed, salted shrimp. It has a very concentrated, pungent odor and flavor that is barely detectable once it has been cooked into one of the recipes in this cookbook. However, it is also made into a dipping sauce for raw vegetables (page 93), which is very strong in flavor. Stored in a cool, dry place, the paste will last indefinitely. Do not refrigerate.

SOY SAUCE

Soy sauce is rarely used in Thailand, where fish sauce predominates. Soy sauce is made by adding mold, brine, and sometimes wheat to soy beans, which are then allowed to ferment for up to 2 years. Depending on the type of soy sauce, dark soy molasses or sugar may be added. Countless brands and types of soy sauce are available; try several to choose the ones you like best.

SOY SAUCE, SWEET

Sweet soy sauce, also called sweet sauce, looks and pours like crude blackstrap molasses and is very similar in taste. At the restaurant it is used sparingly, only to add flavor. It can be found in Thai and Southeast Asian markets. The ingredients include soy beans, salt, water, and sugar.

SZE HSIEN KOW FU

Sze hsien kow fu is a mixture of prepared foods. It contains fried gluten (tofu), bamboo shoots, quail eggs, straw mushrooms, soy sauce, sugar, oil, and salt. At the restaurant it is combined with seafood to make Siam Special (page 139). It is available canned.

TAMARIND, PRESERVED

Tamarind is the ingredient that gives many Thai curries, soups, and sauces that elusive sour flavor. It is the fruit of a tropical leguminous tree whose pods are 3 to 4 inches long and ½ inch wide. Its thin greyish-brown shell encloses a reddish-brown pulp, containing seeds and fiber. Do not mistake these ripe pods for unripened ones, which are sold fresh and frozen, and have a greenish-brown shell. In Thailand they are eaten with a mixture of sugar, salt, and dried chili pepper flakes and are sometimes pounded into the shrimp paste sauce to add tartness. For the recipes, we recommend using the ripe, shelled pods. This form, including the seeds and fiber, comes packaged in 1-pound bricks, called "wet tamarind" or "preserved tamarind." A pure jelly extract is available as well, which we do not recommend because it lacks the texture of the fresh or preserved pulp. You can find all these forms, as well as powdered tamarind, at Southeast Asian markets and East Indian markets. There is no substitute.

In order to use preserved tamarind, the seeds and fiber must first be removed by diluting the tamarind with water. You can either follow the directions given in each recipe to make the required amount, or you can make it in bulk, ahead of time. For bulk preparation, in a large bowl soak the 1-pound brick of preserved tamarind in 4 cups of hot water until soft. Work the tamarind with your hands for 10 to 20 minutes to release all of the pulp. Press it through a fine strainer, or sieve, extracting all of the liquid and pulp, and discard the seeds and fiber. Stored in an airtight plastic container in the refrigerator, it will keep 2 to 3 months.

TANGERINE PEEL, DRIED

The hard, brittle, dried peel of tangerines or oranges is beige on one side and dark brown on the other side. To use it, soak the dried peel in water until soft. In Chinese cooking it adds its sweet citrus flavor to braised and stir-fried dishes. In the cookbook we cook it in the cavity of a roast duck. If it is not available you can dry your own or use fresh peel, after removing the pith. Stored in a sealed container, it will last indefinitely.

TAPIOCA FLOUR (STARCH)

The paste of the cassava root is made into a flour, which is sometimes called tapioca starch. It is ground into a fine white flour, which looks and feels very much like cornstarch. It is used in desserts and also as a thickener. It is available at Asian and Southeast Asian markets.

TAPIOCA PEARL

Tapioca pearl is made from the starchy root of the cassava plant, which used to be considered a garden crop in Thailand but is now grown for export as well. The root is processed, pounded into a paste, and formed into pellets, which are then dried. The pellets come in two sizes, about $\frac{1}{16}$ inch in diameter and about $\frac{3}{16}$ inch in diameter. For Pork Wrapped in Tapioca Pearl (page 49) we recommend the smaller size, although the larger may be substituted. You can purchase it at Asian markets and some health and natural food stores.

TOFU, FIRM

Tofu, which is rich in protein and low in calories, cholesterol, and salt, is made from soybeans. It is cut into blocks of various sizes and is available in soft, regular, and firm textures. At the restaurant the firm type is used. It comes in 19-ounce plastic containers and is packed in water. This type is pre-cut into two pieces about 3 by 3 by $1\frac{1}{4}$ inches each, and we have based the recipes on this size. However, you can use any firm type of tofu, cut into the sizes given in the recipes. Store tofu in the refrigerator, completely immersing it in water. If the water is changed daily, it will keep for 1 to 2 weeks.

TURMERIC

Turmeric is a tiny finger-sized rhizome that is bright orange inside and whose flesh looks like that of a carrot. It is related to ginger. Although it is sometimes available fresh, it is more commonly found in powdered form.

WATER CHESTNUTS

Water chestnuts are readily available in cans at Asian markets and in the Oriental section of the supermarket. Recently, however, fresh water chestnuts have been showing up at the markets in

Chinatown. These underwater tubers have a dark brown skin, which is peeled to reveal its crisp white meat. We recommend using fresh water chestnuts, if available, because they are sweeter and crisper than the canned.

WATERCRESS, CHINESE

Chinese watercress is also called *ong choy* and water spinach. It can be found in Chinese and Southeast Asian markets. Each thin stalk is about 20 inches long with a few long, narrow, pointed leaves growing from the upper third. They are usually tied in large bundles and are sold from early spring to late fall. Before using, trim away the bottom third, and cut the remaining stems into pieces 2 to 3 inches long.

WINTER MELON

Winter melons are large muted-green melons with a waxy exterior that look as if they have been frosted over. They can grow as large as 100 pounds, but when sold commercially range between 10 and 20 pounds. They are sold in Asian markets and some larger produce stores. They are usually cut and sold by the section. Just ask the grocer to slice off the amount you need.

WONTON SKINS, THICK

Wonton skins or wraps are made from a dough of wheat flour, water, eggs, and salt. The dough is repeatedly passed through rollers until the desired thickness is reached, producing one long, continuous sheet. It is then stacked by folding the sheet over onto itself many times, cut into squares and packaged by the pound. For Thai Style Garlic Cookies (page 174) we recommend using "thick" wonton skins, which are about $1/16$ inch thick. The regular thickness may be substituted, but these skins become brittle when fried and do not hold up as well when coated with the garlic sauce.

YELLOW CURRY POWDER

Yellow curry powder is a blend of several pungent ground spices such as cloves, chilies, cumin, coriander seeds, cinnamon, curry leaves, allspice, fenugreek, black peppers, bay leaves, celery seed, nutmeg, onion, and anise but consists mainly of ground turmeric. It is basically the British version of an Indian curry that has become a standard in the Western world and has little to do with the curry pastes given in this cookbook.

Appetizers

FRIED TOFU
(Tofu Tot)

Fried Tofu tastes best piping hot. It has a light, crisp crust and a moist, tender center. Spicy Peanut Sauce provides a wonderful complement to the tofu, which has very little flavor of its own. This dish is easy to prepare, and makes a quick, last-minute appetizer for a party or dinner.

> Oil for deep-frying
> 19 ounces firm tofu (two pieces, each 3 by 3 by 1¼ inches)

In a deep-fryer, heat the oil to 380°.

Lay the tofu flat, and cut each section along the two diagonals, resulting in 4 triangular pieces (8 total). Dry each piece with a paper towel.

Add the tofu to the deep-fryer. Shake the frying basket to keep the tofu from sticking. Deep-fry for 4 minutes, until golden brown and crisp. Remove and drain on paper towels. Arrange the pieces on a platter and serve immediately with Spicy Peanut Sauce (page 88).

> Makes 8 pieces.

SHRIMP AND GROUND PORK TOAST
(Kanom Bung Na Mu)

This recipe can be made in stages. The prawn/pork mixture can be made in advance and kept in the refrigerator for up to 3 days. The mixture can then be spread on the bread and deep-fried just before serving. Thick slices of white bread give the toast body; at the restaurant, the slices are partially frozen so that they will not compress when the mixture is spread. To bring out the flavors of the shrimp and pork, serve the toast with Cucumber Salad.

6 thick slices white bread
2 medium prawns, shelled and deveined
6 ounces lean ground pork
1 tablespoon finely minced garlic
¾ teaspoon ground black pepper
1½ tablespoons fish sauce
½ tablespoon Golden Mountain Sauce
3 tablespoons mung bean thread, soaked in water and cut into
      1-inch lengths
Oil for deep-frying
2 eggs, lightly beaten

Place the bread in the freezer for about an hour, until it is almost com-
    pletely frozen.
Finely chop the prawns. Add the ground pork and continue chopping
    until the prawns and ground pork are thoroughly blended.
Combine the prawn/pork mixture, garlic, black pepper, fish sauce,
    Golden Mountain sauce, and bean thread in a bowl. Allow the mix-
    ture to stand for at least half an hour to blend the flavors.
In a deep-fryer, heat the oil to 380°.
Divide the mixture into 6 portions. Spread one portion evenly over one
    side of a slice of bread. Repeat for the remaining slices.
Working with one slice at a time, dip both sides in the egg to coat
    thoroughly. Starting with the pork side down, deep-fry each side
    for 3 minutes, until golden brown. Drain on paper towels. Repeat
    for the remaining slices.
Cut each slice along the two diagonals, resulting in four triangular pieces.
    Arrange slices on a platter and serve immediately with Cucumber
    Salad (page 76).

    Makes 24 pieces.

 FISH CAKES
(Tot Mun Bla)

This is one of the most popular appetizers served at the restaurant. These deep-fried, spicy, ground-fish patties contain slivered Kaffir
lime leaf, whose sweet citrus flavor is released with each bite. Forming

the patties can be difficult. Wetting your hands will prevent the ground fish from sticking, but it is more important that you make the patties the right thickness. Don't make them too thin, or they will lose their body and become oily in deep-frying. You can purchase the ground fish at most Chinese fish markets (see page 25). The spiced fish mixture can be frozen for 1 to 2 months, if properly sealed. Defrost completely before forming into patties.

> 1 pound ground fish
> 1 cup Blue Lake green beans, thinly sliced into rings
> 1 whole Kaffir lime leaf, thinly sliced into fine slivers
> 5 tablespoons Basic Curry Paste (page 79)
> 1 to 1¼ tablespoons ground cayenne peppers, to taste
> Oil for deep-frying

In a medium bowl combine the ground fish, green beans, lime leaf, curry
    paste (paste only—as little liquid as possible), and cayenne pepper.
In a deep-fryer, heat the oil to 350°.
To make the patties, have a bowl of water handy to wet your hands so
    the ground fish won't stick. Using about 2½ tablespoons of the mix-
    ture, form patties 2 to 2½ inches in diameter and ½ inch thick.
Add several patties to the deep-fryer to cover the surface. Deep-fry for
    about 5 minutes, until the fish cakes are golden brown. Drain on
    paper towels. Repeat for the remaining patties, each time reheating
    the oil to 350°.
Serve immediately with Peanut and Cucumber Sauce (page 76).

> Makes 18 to 20 patties.

 ### BEEF SATAY
(Nuar Satay)

Satay (or *saté*) is an Indonesian word that characterizes a method of cooking. It does not refer to the peanut curry sauce or to the meat, but to the grilling or barbecuing of meat or seafood on a skewer. At Siam Cuisine the beef satay is served with Peanut Curry Sauce (page 92) and Cucumber Salad (page 76) and is by far the most popular dish. The Peanut Curry Sauce and the meat can be prepared ahead of time, with the meat cooked just before serving. This recipe is excellent for outdoor barbecues.

      1 teaspoon grated galanga, fresh or frozen *or* 2 pieces dried
      1¾ cups thick coconut milk
      1 teaspoon fish sauce
      1 teaspoon yellow curry powder
      1 teaspoon ground turmeric
      1¼ to 1½ pounds flank steak
      15 to 20 bamboo skewers
      Aluminum foil (optional)

If dried galanga is used, soak it for 1 to 2 hours in hot tap water. Finely chop, and reserve 2 teaspoons, firmly packed.

To make the marinade, combine the coconut milk, fish sauce, yellow curry powder, turmeric, and galanga in a bowl large enough to hold the beef, and set aside.

Cut the flank steak across the grain, holding the knife at an angle to the cutting surface so that each slice is about 1½ inches wide and ⅛ inch thick. There should be 15 to 20 strips.

Place the beef in the marinade, thoroughly coating each piece. Let it stand in the refrigerator for 2 hours or overnight, until the liquid is absorbed.

Thread each strip of beef lengthwise onto a skewer. You may want to wrap the exposed ends of the skewers with aluminum foil so they won't burn.

Light the charcoal grill to an even, medium-high heat. Adjust the grill to 3 to 4 inches above the coals. Place several skewers at a time on the grill and baste with garlic coconut milk (see below). Cook for 1 minute, until grill marks show on the meat. Turn, and baste the other side. Cook for another minute until done. Remove from grill, and shake off any excess liquid. Repeat for the remaining skewers.

Serve immediately with Cucumber Salad (page 76) and/or Peanut Curry Sauce (page 92).

      Makes 15 to 20 skewers.

Garlic Coconut Milk

      ½ tablespoon oil
      ½ teaspoon finely minced garlic
      ¾ cup thick coconut milk

To prepare the garlic coconut milk, heat a well-seasoned pan over high
heat; add the oil. When oil is hot, add the garlic and sauté until light
brown, being careful not to let it burn. Remove from stove
immediately; the garlic will continue to brown. In a small bowl combine the garlic and oil with the coconut milk. Stir until completely
blended.

FRIED SWEET POTATO
(Mun Tot)

Another popular appetizer, Fried Sweet Potato, is the Thai version of french fries. This dish is easy to prepare and makes a great hit at
any gathering or just to munch on. The potatoes have a hint of coconut
flavoring and are fried until crisp. They are wonderfully complemented
by Spicy Peanut Sauce (page 88).

> 1½ cups rice flour
> ½ cup unsweetened shredded coconut
> ½ cup sugar
> 1¼ teaspoons salt
> ¼ teaspoon red limestone paste
> ¾ cup plus 2 tablespoons thick coconut milk
> 10 sweet potatoes, peeled (approximately 5½ pounds)
> Oil for deep-frying

To make the batter, combine the rice flour, shredded coconut, sugar, salt,
limestone paste, and coconut milk in a large bowl. Set aside.
Cut the sweet potatoes diagonally so that each section is approximately
½ inch thick and 3 inches long. Cut each of these sections
lengthwise into pieces 1 inch wide.
Add the potatoes to the batter, thoroughly coating each piece. Set aside
until oil is ready.
In a deep-fryer, heat the oil to 375°. Add enough potatoes to fill the basket
one quarter full. Cook 5 to 6 minutes, until golden brown. Shake
the basket occasionally so the pieces don't stick together. Drain on
paper towels. Repeat for remaining potatoes.
Serve immediately with Spicy Peanut Sauce (page 88).

Serves 8 to 10.

CHARCOAL-BROILED CALAMARI
(Bla Murk Bing)

At the restaurant, Charcoal-Broiled Calamari is a very popular appetizer. Before the calamari is marinated, it is parboiled to remove any fishy smell, to hold in the flavor, and to make it tender when grilled. Don't over-marinate the calamari—the spices will eat away at the flesh, causing it to lose its tender crunchiness. While grilling, flip it only once to minimize shrinkage. Serve as an appetizer or as a main dish.

> 12 medium to large calamari (1 to 1½ pounds)
> 2 teaspoons grated galanga, fresh or frozen *or* 2 pieces dried
> 1 cup thick coconut milk
> 1 teaspoon turmeric
> 1 teaspoon fish sauce
> ¼ teaspoon yellow curry powder (optional)
> 24 bamboo skewers
> Garlic Coconut Milk (page 42)

Clean the calamari (page 18). Cut the body sections and the base of the tentacles in half lengthwise so that you have identical sections. Each body section should be about 1½ inches wide and 5 to 6 inches long.

Using a large strainer to hold the calamari pieces, parboil for 3 seconds, until the calamari becomes opaque. Drain well. Do this step in several portions so the temperature of the water doesn't drop too much; it must be at a full boil.

If dried galanga is used, soak it for 1 to 2 hours in hot tap water. Finely chop, and reserve 2 teaspoons, firmly packed.

Combine the coconut milk, turmeric, fish sauce, grated galanga, and yellow curry powder in a medium bowl. Add the calamari pieces and coat thoroughly.

Thread the body sections onto skewers, topping each with a section of tentacles, and place in a baking pan. Pour the remaining marinade over the skewered calamari and let it stand for 2 hours.

Light the charcoal grill to an even, high heat. Adjust the grill to 3 to 4 inches above the coals. Place several skewers at a time on the grill and baste with the garlic coconut milk. Cook for 45 seconds, until grill marks show on the calamari. Turn, and baste the other side. Cook for another 45 seconds, until done. Remove from grill, and shake off any excess liquid. Repeat for the remaining skewers. Serve immediately with Green Chili Sauce (page 87).

Makes 24 skewers.

 ## CHARCOAL-BROILED FISH
(Bla Chin Bing)

Charcoal-Broiled Fish is best grilled the same day it is marinated. It may be kept in the refrigerator overnight, but it should not be kept any longer than that. After the fish has been skewered, keep it in the refrigerator until you are ready to grill it. Serve as an appetizer or as a main course.

> 2 tablespoons butter
> ½ teaspoon ground white pepper
> 2 tablespoons chopped onion
> ½ cup thick coconut milk
> 2 pounds rock cod filet (approximately 4 filets), or other firm-fleshed fish filet, patted dry and cut into 1-inch squares
> 12 bamboo skewers
> Garlic Coconut Milk (page 42)

In a well-seasoned pan, melt the butter over medium-high heat. Add the white pepper and onion, and sauté until the onion is browned and fragrant.

In a medium bowl combine the butter mixture and coconut milk. Cool to room temperature. Add the fish, and let stand for 20 minutes.

Thread 5 pieces of fish per skewer and place skewers in a baking pan. Pour the remaining marinade over the fish and refrigerate until ready to grill.

Light the charcoal grill to an even, high heat. Adjust the grill to 3 to 4 inches above the coals. Place several skewers at a time on the grill and baste with garlic coconut milk. Cook 3 minutes, until the fish no longer sticks to the grill. Turn, and baste the other side. Cook for another 3 minutes until done. Repeat for the remaining skewers.

Serve immediately with Green Chili Sauce (page 87).

Makes 12 skewers.

CHARCOAL-BROILED SCALLOPS
(Scallops Bing)

Use large scallops for this recipe; they hold up better on the grill.

2 tablespoons butter
½ teaspoon ground white pepper
2 tablespoons chopped onion
24 fresh, medium button mushrooms, stems removed
36 large scallops (approximately 1¾ pounds), patted dry
½ cup thick coconut milk
12 bamboo skewers
Garlic Coconut Milk (page 42)

In a well-seasoned pan, melt the butter over medium heat. Add the white pepper, onion, and mushrooms and sauté until the onion is browned.

In a medium bowl combine the butter mixture and coconut milk. Cool to room temperature. Add the scallops and let stand for 20 minutes.

Thread 3 scallops and 2 mushrooms per skewer, alternating the pieces, and place skewers in a baking pan. Pour the remaining marinade over the scallops and refrigerate until ready to grill.

Light the charcoal grill to an even, high heat. Adjust the grill to 3 to 4 inches above the coals. Place several skewers at a time on the grill and baste with garlic coconut milk. Cook 2 to 3 minutes. Turn, and baste the other side. Cook another 3 minutes until done. Repeat for the remaining skewers.

Serve immediately with Green Chili Sauce (page 87).

Makes 12 skewers.

THAI CRISP-FRIED RICE THREADS
(Mee Krob)

In the marketplaces of Thailand, Mee Krob is made by combining a pre-made sauce with the other ingredients at the time the order is placed. This recipe also uses a sauce that is made in advance with ample amount for two recipes. When deep-frying the rice noodles, they must be completely cooked. Make sure the oil is hot by testing a few noodles before frying the rest. It should puff up light, crisp, and opaque, not hard and chewy.

The Mee Krob sauce should be a lumpy, deep red mixture almost as thick as honey. It is tart and sweet and will keep for about a month in the refrigerator. Bring it to room temperature before using. Food coloring is added to the sauce for presentation only, and may be omitted.

Mee Krob Sauce
> 1 ounce preserved tamarind
> 3 tablespoons hot water
> 1 head preserved garlic
> 1 tablespoon liquid from preserved garlic
> 26 small marshmallows
> ¼ cup plus 1 tablespoon brown sugar, firmly packed
> 2 tablespoons palm sugar
> ¼ cup plus 1 tablespoon white sugar
> ½ cup plus 2 tablespoons white vinegar
> ½ tablespoon bean sauce
> ¼ teaspoon red food coloring (optional)
> ¼ teaspoon yellow food coloring (optional)
> 1 tablespoon water
> ½ tablespoon salt

In a small bowl soak the tamarind in 3 tablespoons hot water for 30 minutes, until soft. Work the tamarind with your hands for 5 minutes to release the pulp. Press pulp through a strainer. Squeeze out all the liquid and pulp, and discard the twigs and seeds. Reserve 1½ tablespoons.

Discard the outer skin and stem of the preserved garlic. Thinly slice the whole head.

In a small saucepan place the tamarind, preserved garlic, its liquid, marshmallows, sugars, white vinegar, bean sauce, food colorings (if used), 1 tablespoon water, and salt. Bring to a boil over high heat, then lower to medium high. Cook for 10 minutes, stirring constantly. Be careful not to let the sauce scorch.

To test for the right consistency, allow the sauce to drip from a spoon and cool slightly. When it is sticky to the touch, almost forming threads, it is ready. Remove from heat and allow to cool.

Makes approximately ¾ cup.

Mee Krob

> 4 raw medium prawns (approximately 2 to 3 ounces), shelled and deveined
> Oil for deep-frying
> 2 ounces rice threads *or* rice stick noodles
> 1 beaten egg
> 5 ounces firm tofu, cut into 2 pieces, each 1 by 1½ by 2½ inches
> 18 small marshmallows
> 6 tablespoons Mee Krob sauce (see above)
> 2 green onions, cut into 2-inch lengths
> 3 ounces bean sprouts

Using a large strainer to hold the prawns, parboil for 2 seconds. The prawns should be just turning pink on the edges. Do not overcook; the cooking process will be completed later. Drain well and set aside.

In a deep-fryer, heat the oil to 400°.

To deep-fry the rice threads, first separate them in a large paper bag. Add a small handful to the hot oil. If the oil is hot enough, the rice thread will puff up instantly. Quickly remove from the oil, and drain on paper towels. Be careful not to let them burn. The darkest they should be is a light golden color. If they become dark brown too fast, reduce the heat a little and continue. Repeat for the remainder of the rice threads, each time reheating the oil to 400°. Set aside.

Reheat the same oil to 400°. To deep-fry the egg, slowly pour it through a strainer to create long strands on the surface of the oil. Cook until crisp and golden brown, carefully turning once. Remove from the oil, drain on paper towels, and set aside.

Reheat the same oil to 400°. To deep-fry the tofu, pat the pieces dry and fry for 3 minutes until golden brown and crisp. Remove from the oil, and drain on paper towels. Allow to cool, and slice into pieces ¼ inch thick. Set aside.

To cook the Mee Krob, heat a large wok over high heat. Add the prawns, fried tofu, marshmallows, and Mee Krob Sauce. Cook for 1 minute, allowing the marshmallows to melt. Stir constantly as the mixture begins to boil and thicken. Gradually coat the wok with the mixture until it reaches half-way up the sides, being careful not to let it burn. Quickly add the green onions and deep-fried noodles. Gently stir to coat thoroughly, breaking the noodles as little as possible. Transfer to a large platter and garnish with the fried eggs. Place the bean sprouts to one side.

Serves 4.

PORK WRAPPED IN TAPIOCA PEARL
(Saku Sai Mu)

The filling for the Pork Wrapped in Tapioca Pearl is very strong tasting. Its texture and piquant flavor provide a nice contrast to the soft, sticky, bland tapioca wrapping. The dumplings are steamed and then rolled in a penetrating garlic oil to enhance the already intense flavors. This dish is usually prepared with ground pork, but chicken may be substituted. For the best texture, use chopped instead of ground chicken. Stuffing the dumplings will take some time and practice, so be patient. Make sure the tapioca is moist and pasty, with undissolved pearls still visible. If the tapioca is too dry, it will become tough when cooked. The filling may be prepared in advance and kept in the freezer for up to 2 months, if properly sealed. These dumplings may be served as a snack or appetizer.

Pork Filling

½ tablespoon chopped coriander root
½ cup raw peanuts (approximately 2½ ounces)
1½ tablespoons oil
½ tablespoon minced garlic
9 ounces lean ground pork (approximately 1 cup)
½ cup rinsed, finely chopped brine-cured radish (approximately 3¼ ounces), lightly packed
½ cup finely chopped shallots
½ cup sugar
2 tablespoons Golden Mountain sauce or fish sauce
½ teaspoon ground white pepper

Tapioca

2 cups small tapioca pearl (approximately 12 ounces)
3 tablespoons tapioca flour
1½ to 2 cups boiling water

Ingredients to complete the recipe

1 banana leaf
2 tablespoons finely minced garlic
½ cup oil
4 iceberg lettuce leaves, washed and drained
20 Fresh Thai chili peppers
Leaves from 1 bunch fresh coriander
1 bunch green onions

To make the filling:

In a mortar, pound the coriander roots to a paste. Set aside.

Dry-roast the peanuts in a skillet for 10 minutes over medium-low heat until evenly browned, flipping frequently. Cool to room temperature. In a mortar, pound peanuts into small pieces. Set aside.

Heat a well-seasoned pan or wok over high heat and add the oil. When oil is hot add the garlic and coriander roots and stir-fry until the garlic is browned. Add the ground pork and stir-fry until the pinkness is gone. Add the brine-cured radish, shallots, sugar, Golden Mountain sauce, white pepper, and peanuts. Stir-fry for 10 to 15 minutes, until the sugar has browned, being careful not to burn the mixture. Remove from the stove and set aside.

Assembling and cooking:

In a small bowl combine the tapioca pearl and tapioca flour. Gradually add 1½ cups of the boiling water, stirring to moisten and partially dissolve the tapioca pearl. Knead the tapioca for about 3 minutes until it becomes very glutinous and holds together. It should have a very pasty consistency. If it begins to feel dry and crumbly while you are working with it, gradually add more boiling water and knead again.

Have a bowl of water handy to keep your hands moist to prevent the tapioca from sticking. Roll ½ tablespoon of the tapioca into a ball and flatten it into a circle with the fingers and thumb of one hand so that the tapioca pearl is one layer thick. Place 1 teaspoon of the filling in the center of the circle. Bring up the edges and seal to form a ball. Place in a streamer tray lined with banana leaf. Do not allow the balls to touch. Repeat with the remaining filling.

Steam for 25 minutes until the tapioca pearl is completely transparent and does not appear to be covered with white dots. Repeat until all the dumplings are steamed.

In the meantime, heat the ½ cup of oil in a skillet over medium-high heat. Add the garlic and fry until light brown, being careful not to let it burn. Remove from stove immediately; the garlic will continue to brown. Allow to cool.

When the tapioca is done, remove the dumplings from the steamer and place them directly in the garlic oil. Thoroughly coat each one.

Arrange on a platter over a bed of lettuce. Garnish with the Thai chili peppers, coriander leaves, and green onions.

Makes approximately 55.

THAI APPETIZER
(Gai Saam Yang)

Even though meals in Thailand are served family-style, this dish comes very close to what we call appetizers. In Thailand it is usually served with alcoholic beverages, similar to "pupus" in Hawaii. To eat it, put one or more pieces of each item in the palm of your hand and pop them directly into your mouth for a sensational burst of flavors. To add heat, nibble on a Thai chili pepper. The only problem is that you might get full before dinner is ready.

>   1 to 2 medium limes
>   ½ cup raw peanuts (approximately 2½ ounces)
>   ½ cup medium dried shrimp (approximately 1½ ounces)
>   18 to 24 thin slices fresh ginger, ¾ inch in diameter (approximately ½ to ¾ ounce)
>   1 large stalk lemon grass, thinly sliced
>   3 small shallots, thinly sliced (approximately 1½ to 2 ounces)
>   18 to 24 Thai chili peppers (optional)

Cut each lime into about 12 triangular sections, each with a section of rind attached. Set aside.

Dry roast the raw peanuts over medium-low heat for about 10 minutes, flipping constantly so that they brown evenly. Set aside to cool.

Arrange the lime, peanuts, dried shrimp, ginger, lemon grass, shallots, and Thai chili peppers in sections on a serving platter.

Serves 4.

Soups

CHICKEN STOCK
(Nam Thom Graduk Gai)

This all-purpose chicken stock can be made in advance and kept in the refrigerator for up to five days. If boiled every four to five days, it will keep longer; or it can be frozen. Each time you bone a chicken, put the bones in the freezer until you have accumulated enough to complete the recipe. You can use whole chicken, but after boiling, the meat will be completely flavorless, so don't plan on using it in another recipe. At the restaurant, chicken stock is made fresh every day. An onion is cooked with the bones to give the stock sweetness and to reduce its smell. It is simmered at a very low boil to yield a clear broth.

> 1 medium yellow onion, peeled
> 10 cups water, or enough to cover
> Bones from 8 chickens *or* 1 whole 3½- to 4-pound chicken

Place the onion and water in a stockpot and bring to a boil over high heat.
Add the bones and bring to a vigorous boil. Reduce the heat to low, cover, and simmer for 3 hours.
Allow the broth to cool. Strain, reserving only the liquid. Skim the rendered fat from the surface.

> Makes about 8 cups.

THAI CHICKEN SOUP
(Thom Kha Gai)

Thai Chicken Soup is the most popular soup served at the Siam Cuisine. It is not a typical chicken soup, combining as it does the sweetness of coconut milk with the tanginess of lime juice. To add another dimension of flavors to the soup, thin slices of fresh galanga are added, which are meant to be eaten.

3-inch section fresh or frozen galanga *or* 1 ounce dried

1 cup fresh Chicken Stock (page 53)

1 stalk lemon grass, cut into 3-inch lengths and crushed

1 whole Kaffir lime leaf *or* 1 lime leaf (optional)

¾ teaspoon salt

¾ teaspoon sugar

6 ounces boned, skinned chicken breast, thinly sliced (approximately ⅔ cup)

8 slices bamboo shoots (1½ to 2 ounces)

½ cup thick coconut milk

2 teaspoons fresh lime juice

2 sprigs fresh coriander

Slice about ½ inch of the galanga into 15 paper-thin pieces. Crush the remaining section of galanga with the handle of a knife and set aside. (If dried galanga is used, boil it in 1½ cups of water for 10 to 15 minutes. Place the galanga and water in a blender and grind into a paste. Save the galanga water by straining the paste, squeezing out as much liquid as possible.)

Combine the Chicken Stock, lemon grass, Kaffir lime leaf, salt, and sugar, and the sliced and crushed galanga (or the galanga water) in a medium saucepan. Reduce over high heat until about ½ cup of liquid remains.

Add the chicken, bamboo shoots, and coconut milk in order. Boil for 2 minutes, until chicken is done.

Remove from the stove. Add the lime juice and stir. Garnish with the coriander and serve immediately.

Serves 4.

HOT AND SOUR PRAWN SOUP
(Thom Yum Gung)

This tart and tangy soup makes a wonderful beginning to any dinner—one sip and your taste buds will beg for more. The broth has an aromatic sweetness, which enhances the "hot" from spicy chili oil, and the "sour" from lemon grass and lime juice. If you use jumbo prawns, don't shell them; they can be eaten as you would lobster tails.

In Thailand these days, it is common for coconut milk to be added to the broth, but at the restaurant it is made the old-fashioned way, without coconut milk.

> 10 raw medium prawns, shelled and deveined *or* 4 jumbo
>   prawns (4 to 6 per pound)
> 2 cups fresh Chicken Stock (page 53)
> 2 tablespoons fish sauce
> 1 tablespoon Spicy Chili Oil for Hot and Sour Soup (page 90)
> 8 medium button mushrooms
> 3- to 4-inch piece lemon grass, crushed
> 1 whole Kaffir lime leaf *or* 3 lime leaves (optional)
> 2 sprigs coriander, lightly chopped
> 3 teaspoons fresh lime juice

Using a large strainer to hold the prawns, parboil for 3 seconds until they turn pink on the edges. Do not overcook—the cooking process will be completed later. Drain well and set aside.

In a medium saucepan bring the Chicken Stock, fish sauce, Spicy Chili Oil, mushrooms, lemon grass, and Kaffir lime leaf to a vigorous boil over high heat. Immediately turn off the heat and add the prawns, coriander, and lime juice. Stir and serve immediately.

Serves 4.

HOT AND SOUR VEGETABLE SOUP
WITH PRAWNS
(Gang Som Pak)

This medium-hot soup is different from Hot and Sour Prawn Soup in that it gets its tartness from tamarind rather than from lime juice. It is usually cooked with green papaya, but any vegetable may be substituted. I often use napa cabbage. In Thailand a whole fresh-water fish is boiled to make the stock. The fish is then pounded in a mortar and added with the vegetables. In this recipe fish filet is used only to heighten the flavor of the chicken stock; the prawns are the primary seafood. This soup can be served either hot or at room temperature, as the main course or as one of many.

5 ounces preserved tamarind

1¼ cups hot water

7 dried red chili peppers, 2 to 3 inches long *or*

      7 dried cayenne peppers *and*

      1 dried New Mexico chili pepper for color

4 cups fresh Chicken Stock (page 53)

1 medium yellow onion, peeled

3½ ounces rock cod filet *or* any firm-fleshed fish filet

1 medium clove garlic

½ teaspoon salt

2 small shallots, peeled (approximately 1 ounce)

1 teaspoon shrimp paste

¼ cup plus 1 teaspoon fish sauce

¼ teaspoon sugar

1 pound napa cabbage, sliced into pieces 2 inches wide *or*

      1 pound green beans, cut into pieces 2 inches long *or*

      1 pound bean sprouts

10 large raw prawns (shelling and deveining are optional)

In a small bowl soak the tamarind in the hot water for 30 minutes until soft. Work the tamarind with your hands for 10 minutes to release the pulp. Press it through a strainer, extracting all the liquid and pulp. Discard the twigs and seeds. Reserve ½ cup.

Soak the red chilies in warm water for about 15 minutes, until soft. Remove and discard the stems and seeds. Set aside.

Place the Chicken Stock and yellow onion in a stockpot and bring to a vigorous boil over high heat. Add the rock cod. Lower the heat to medium low and boil for 10 minutes without stirring. Turn off the heat and set aside.

Place the chilies, garlic, salt, shallots, and shrimp paste in a mortar or blender. Pound or grind into fine pieces. (If using a blender, add 1 cup of the Chicken Stock above to aid in grinding.) This mixture does not have to be as fine as curry paste. Set aside.

Discard the onion and remove the fish from the stock. Discard any bones. Add the fish to the mortar or blender and pound or grind into very small pieces, combining with the other ground ingredients. Add a couple of tablespoons of stock, if necessary, while pounding the fish to make sure there are no large chunks.

Empty the contents of the mortar or blender into the stockpot and stir.

Add the tamarind, fish sauce, and sugar, and bring the soup to a
vigorous boil over high heat.

Add the napa cabbage or green beans, cover, and bring back up to a
vigorous boil. Add the prawns, stir, and turn off the heat. If using
bean sprouts, add the prawns to the vigorously boiling broth, turn
off the heat, and add the bean sprouts. Serve immediately.

Serves 6.

 ## PORK SPARERIB SOUP WITH WINTER MELON
(Fang Thom Graduk Mu)

This mild soup is similar to the Chinese version. Ground pork
may be substituted for spareribs. When cooking the ground pork, start
with cooled chicken stock. To keep the broth clear, simmer at a very low
boil.

1¾ pounds pork spareribs *or*
    10 ounces lean ground pork
    1 medium clove garlic, minced
    1 tablespoon fish sauce
6 cups fresh Chicken Stock (page 53)
¼ cup dried shrimp
3-pound section winter melon
5 large cloves garlic, peeled and smashed
¼ teaspoon ground white pepper
¼ teaspoon sugar
1 teaspoon Golden Mountain sauce
4 tablespoons fish sauce
3 green onions, cut into 2-inch lengths
5 whole coriander plants, lightly chopped

Cut the spareribs into individual ribs and then into 2-inch lengths, or
have the butcher cut them for you. Or, if you are using ground pork,
combine it with the minced garlic and fish sauce in a small bowl.
Allow it to stand for 20 minutes. Form into 1½-inch meatballs.

Place the pork, Chicken Stock, and dried shrimp in a stockpot, cover and
bring to a boil over high heat. Reduce the heat to low and simmer
for 7 minutes, until the meat has shrunk on the bones.

Peel the rind from the winter melon. Scrape out and discard the pulp
and seeds, and cut into 2-inch cubes.

Add the winter melon, garlic, white pepper, sugar, Golden Mountain
sauce, and fish sauce to the stockpot. Cover and bring to a boil over
high heat. Reduce the heat to low and simmer for 25 minutes, until
the melon becomes transparent. Remove from heat and skim off
rendered fat. Add the green onions and coriander; serve immediately.

Serves 8 to 10.

 ## STUFFED BITTER MELON SOUP
(Mara Pat Sai Mu)

This recipe is one that Kwan's mother and father often made
at home. As a child Kwan disliked bitter melon, but since coming to
America, she has grown to like it very much. The soup is a mild blend
of flavors and is very satisfying. Cook the bitter melon until well done,
simmering at a very low boil.

1½ ounces dried black mushrooms
1½ pounds bitter melon
2 medium cloves garlic, finely minced
¼ teaspoon ground white pepper
3 tablespoons plus 1 teaspoon fish sauce
1 teaspoon water
1 pound lean ground pork
4 cups fresh Chicken Stock (page 53)
1 tablespoon Golden Mountain sauce
¼ teaspoon sugar

In a small bowl soak the black mushrooms for 20 minutes, until tender.
Remove and discard the stems. Set the mushrooms aside.

Trim the ends of the bitter melon and cut them into 3-inch sections. Scoop
out and discard the white pulp and seeds from inside each section.
Set the bitter melon aside.

In a medium bowl combine the minced garlic, ⅛ teaspoon of the white
pepper, 1 tablespoon + 1 teaspoon of the fish sauce, the water, and
the ground pork. Allow the mixture to stand for 20 minutes to blend
the flavors.

Stuff each section of bitter melon with the pork mixture, packing firmly, and set aside. If there is any ground pork left, form it into 1½-inch meatballs and set aside.

Place the Chicken Stock, Golden Mountain sauce, sugar, the rest of the white pepper, the rest of the fish sauce, and the meat balls, if any, in a stockpot. Cover and bring to a vigorous boil over high heat.

Add the stuffed bitter melon sections, cover, and bring to a boil again. Turn the heat to low and simmer for 10 minutes.

Add the black mushrooms to the stockpot. Turn the bitter melon at the same time to cook the pork evenly. Simmer for another 20 minutes, until the pork is well done. Skim off the rendered fat and serve immediately.

> Serves 6.

 BITTER MELON SOUP WITH SPARERIBS
(Mara Thom Graduk Mu)

This soup is similar to Stuffed Bitter Melon Soup (page 58) and is very easy to prepare. It has a mild, full-bodied broth, with a smooth blending of flavors. The bitter melon is cooked until well done, which dilutes much of its bitterness. To insure that the broth will remain clear and not turn cloudy, simmer it over low heat.

> 1½ pounds pork spareribs
> 6 cups fresh Chicken Stock (page 53)
> 1½ pounds bitter melon
> 3 medium cloves garlic, crushed
> 1 tablespoon Golden Mountain sauce
> 4 tablespoons fish sauce
> ¼ teaspoon ground white pepper
> ¼ teaspoon sugar

Cut the spareribs into individual ribs and then into 2-inch lengths, or have the butcher cut them for you. Place the ribs and Chicken Stock in a stockpot, cover, and bring to a boil over high heat. Reduce the heat to low and simmer at a low boil for 7 minutes, until the meat has shrunk on the bones.

Slice the bitter melon in half lengthwise. Scrape out and discard the white pulp and seeds from the center of each half. Cut into 2-inch pieces and set aside.

Add the bitter melon, garlic, Golden Mountain sauce, fish sauce, white pepper, and sugar to the stockpot. Cover and bring back to a boil over high heat. Reduce the heat to low and simmer for 25 minutes. Skim the rendered fat from the broth and serve immediately.

Serves 6 to 8.

 ## CHINESE OKRA SOUP
(Gang Rieng Buap)

Chinese Okra Soup is a country-style dish often served at family meals. If you can find fresh ingredients, especially the lemon basil, this is a lovely soup; but all of the ingredients must be fresh. This soup is very delicate and aromatic and must be eaten on the first day. If lemon basil and Chinese okra are not available, use a bunch of spinach in their place.

> 1 large firm Chinese okra (approximately 8 ounces)
> 15 white peppercorns *or* ½ teaspoon ground white pepper
> 3 tablespoons frozen *krachai*, thinly sliced (approximately ⅘ ounce)
> 2 small shallots, thinly sliced (approximately 1 ounce)
> ⅓ cup large dried shrimp (approximately 1 ounce)
> 8 to 9 straw or button mushrooms (approximately 3½ ounces)
> 10 fresh baby corn
> 2 teaspoons shrimp paste
> 2 cups water
> 10 to 15 medium prawns, shelled and deveined (approximately 8 ounces)
> Dash of fish sauce to taste
> 50 to 80 leaves lemon basil (2 bunches)

Peel the ridges of the Chinese okra. Slice into 1½-inch wedge-shaped pieces and set aside.

Place the white peppercorns, *krachai*, shallots, and dried shrimp in a mortar or blender and pound or grind into a paste. (If using a blender, add ½ cup of the water to process.)

Empty the contents of the mortar or blender into a medium saucepan. Add the Chinese okra, mushrooms, baby corn, shrimp paste, and remaining water. Bring to a boil over medium-high heat and cook for 5 to 6 minutes, until the okra is done. Remove from the heat, add the prawns and lemon basil, and stir. Taste soup and add the fish sauce. Serve immediately.

Serves 4.

 ## CLEAR FISH SOUP
(Thom Yum Bla Nam Sai)

Clear Fish Soup is quick and easy to prepare. This very sour, salty, and pungent soup can serve as a main course or as one of many. Kwan uses rock cod or bass, but any type of firm-fleshed fish will do. To prevent the broth from getting cloudy and the fish from overcooking, boil the fish without a cover and turn off the heat as soon as it reaches a boil.

> 7 small shallots (approximately 4½ ounces)
> 5 jalapeño or serrano chili peppers
> 6 cups fresh Chicken Stock (page 53)
> 3 stalks lemon grass, crushed and cut into 4-inch lengths
> 3-inch section fresh or frozen galanga, crushed *or* ½ ounce dried
> 5 whole Kaffir lime leaves *or* 7 lime leaves
> Roots and leaves of ⅓ bunch fresh coriander
> 2-pound whole rock cod or bass, cut into 1-inch thick steaks
> 7 tablespoons fresh lime juice (save rinds)
> 3½ tablespoons fish sauce

Leaving skins intact, charcoal grill the shallots for 8 to 10 minutes and the jalapeño chili peppers for 4 to 5 minutes over high heat until they are slightly tender, turning to cook evenly. Remove from the grill and discard the charred skins of the shallots. Crush the shallots and jalapeño peppers slightly to release their juices and set aside.

In a large saucepan bring the Chicken Stock, lemon grass, galanga, Kaffir lime leaves, and coriander roots to a boil over high heat.

Immediately add the fish, making sure it is completely covered by the broth. Bring to a boil again without a cover; turn off the heat immediately. Add the jalapeños, shallots, lime juice, lime rinds, and fish sauce.

Garnish with the coriander and serve immediately. Remove the lime rinds after 10 or 15 minutes. If they are left in too long, the broth will become bitter.

Serves 4 to 6.

PLAIN RICE SOUP
(Kow Thom)

In typical Thai homes Plain Rice Soup is served for breakfast. It is usually eaten with something very strong in flavor like Sweet Pork (page 102), Salty Beef (page 111), or Thai Egg Foo Yung (page 102), along with dried shrimp and preserved radish to offset its blandness.

    1 cup cooked, day-old rice
    3 cups water

Place the rice and water in a small saucepan and bring to a boil. Serve immediately.

Serves 1 to 2.

CHICKEN RICE SOUP
(Kow Thom Gai)

In Bangkok, Chicken Rice Soup is available any time, night or day. It differs from Plain Rice Soup in that it is eaten as a meal and does not have to be supplemented with other foods.

    ½ tablespoon oil
    ¼ teaspoon minced garlic
    ½ teaspoon preserved cabbage
    3 cups fresh Chicken Stock (page 53)
    2½ ounces boned, skinned chicken breast, sliced into thin, bite-
        sized pieces (approximately ¼ cup)
    1 tablespoon fish sauce
    1 teaspoon Golden Mountain sauce

¾ cup cooked, day-old rice
1 small green onion, thinly sliced
Leaves from 4 sprigs fresh coriander
Leaves from 3 to 4 stalks Chinese celery
Dash of ground white pepper

Place the oil and garlic in a well-seasoned pan. Brown the garlic over high heat, being careful not to let it burn. Remove the garlic and set aside.

Place the preserved cabbage, Chicken Stock, chicken, fish sauce, and Golden Mountain sauce in a saucepan. Bring to a boil over high heat, then reduce the heat to low. Simmer for 2 minutes until the chicken is done. Add the rice and turn the heat to high. When the broth begins to steam, remove from the stove and pour into a serving bowl.

Garnish with the green onions, coriander, Chinese celery, browned garlic, and white pepper in order. Serve immediately.

Serves 1.

Salads and Vegetables

 PRAWN SALAD
(Pla Gung)

Prawn Salad is a wonderful combination of sour, salty, and hot. In Thailand, the prawns are often added to the salad raw. At the restaurant and in this recipe, the prawns are partially cooked; lime juice completes the cooking process. Hotness is controlled by the amount and strength of the Sriracha Chili Sauce used. In Thailand, crushed fresh chili peppers are added to the salad.

> 10 medium prawns, shelled and deveined (approximately ⅓ pound)
> 5 teaspoons fresh lime juice
> 2 to 3 teaspoons Sriracha chili sauce
> 1¼ teaspoons fish sauce
> Leaves from 6 sprigs fresh coriander
> 20 medium mint leaves
> 2 teaspoons thinly sliced lemon grass, firmly packed
> 3 to 4 thin slices red onion
> Iceberg or romaine lettuce, washed and drained

Using a large strainer to hold the prawns, parboil for 3 seconds until they turn pink on the edges. Be careful not to overcook them; the cooking process will be completed later. Drain well and place in a medium bowl.

Add the lime juice and stir, completely coating the prawns. Allow to stand for a few minutes.

Add the Sriracha chili sauce and fish sauce; stir. Add the coriander leaves, mint leaves, lemon grass, and red onion. Stir to thoroughly coat all ingredients.

Arrange several whole leaves of lettuce on a platter. Coarsely chop 2 to 3 leaves and place on top. Serve the mixture on the bed of lettuce, garnished with coriander leaves.

Serves 2.

CALAMARI SALAD
(Yum Bla Murk)

Calamari Salad is one of the most popular salads at Siam Cuisine. It has a cooling minty flavor, which is enhanced by the sour and salty flavors of the dressing, but it can be very hot, depending on the sharpness and the amount of ginger used and on the strength of the Sriracha chili sauce. The calamari is parboiled for just an instant to retain its tender crunchiness. Don't overcook it, or it will become tough and chewy.

> 4 medium calamari (approximately 5 to 6 ounces)
> 3 to 4 thin slices fresh ginger
> 3 teaspoons fresh lime juice
> 2 to 3 teaspoons Sriracha chili sauce
> 1 teaspoon fish sauce
> 3 to 4 thin slices red onion
> Leaves from 6 sprigs fresh coriander
> 15 medium mint leaves, cut in half
> Iceberg or romaine lettuce, washed and drained

Clean the calamari, following the instructions on page 18. Cut the body crosswise into 1-inch rings. Using a large strainer to hold the calamari rings and tentacles, parboil for 5 seconds until they become firm and opaque. Drain well and set aside.

Cut the slices of ginger into julienne pieces and set aside.

Mix together the calamari and lime juice in a medium bowl. Add the Sriracha chili sauce and fish sauce and mix. Add the ginger, red onion slices, coriander leaves, and mint leaves. Mix well to thoroughly coat all the ingredients.

Serve on a bed of lettuce as in the Prawn Salad (page 65).

Serves 2.

BEEF SALAD I
(Yum Yai)

This is one of many beef salads in the Thai cuisine. At Siam Cuisine the center section of a chuck roast is charcoal-grilled and then sliced as needed for Yum Yai and Yum Nuar (page 68). The unused portion can be frozen or refrigerated for 4 or 5 days. Yum Yai is moderately hot and is served warm.

> Center section of a chuck roast, cut along the membrane holding the sections together.
> 2 dried cayenne peppers
> 1 tablespoon fresh Chicken Stock (page 53)
> 1 teaspoon Golden Mountain sauce
> 3 teaspoons fresh lime juice
> 1½ teaspoons Kwan's Sweet and Sour Sauce (page 87)
> ½ medium tomato, sliced into wedges
> 3 to 4 thin slices red onion
> ½ cucumber, peeled and sliced ⅛ to ¼ inch thick
> Leaves from 12 sprigs fresh coriander
> 1 tablespoon fish sauce
> Iceberg or romaine lettuce, washed and drained

Charcoal-grill the chuck roast over high heat to sear in the juices and to give the meat a nice charcoal flavor. Grill for 2 to 3 minutes on each side, leaving the center raw. Remove from the grill and slice thinly across the grain until you have cut 4 ounces; set aside. Store the uncut portion.

In a skillet dry-roast the cayenne peppers over medium heat until they turn a deep red, being careful not to let them burn. Using a mortar, grind them into small flakes. Reserve ½ teaspoon, and set aside.

In a small saucepan bring the Chicken Stock and Golden Mountain sauce to a boil over high heat. Add the beef and cook until it is heated and the liquid is absorbed. The beef should be medium done. Quickly remove the pan from the stove and add the ground cayenne peppers, lime juice, and Kwan's Sweet and Sour Sauce. Mix thoroughly. Add the tomato slices, red onion, cucumber, coriander, and fish sauce in order. Mix well to combine the flavors.

Serve immediately on a bed of lettuce as in the Prawn Salad (page 65).

Serves 2.

BEEF SALAD II
(Yum Nuar)

Yum Nuar uses the same type of beef as Yum Yai. It combines the sour and salty and medium-hot flavors to which mint leaves are added for a refreshing, satisfying taste. It is also served warm.

> Center section of a chuck roast, cut along the membrane hold-
>   ing the sections together
> 1 teaspoon uncooked rice
> 2 dried cayenne peppers
> 1 tablespoon fresh Chicken Stock (page 53)
> 1 teaspoon Golden Mountain sauce
> 3 teaspoons fresh lime juice
> 1 tablespoon thinly sliced green onion
> 24 medium mint leaves
> Leaves from 14 sprigs fresh coriander
> 4 teaspoons fish sauce
> Iceberg or romaine lettuce, washed and drained

Charcoal-grill the chuck roast over high heat to sear in the juices and give the meat a nice charcoal flavor. Grill for 2 to 3 minutes on each side, leaving the center raw. Remove from the grill and slice thinly across the grain until you have cut 5 to 6 ounces; set aside. Store the uncut portion.

In a skillet dry-roast the rice over high heat until brown. Grind in a mortar and set aside.

In the same skillet, dry-roast the cayenne peppers over medium heat until deep red, being careful not to let them burn. Grind them into small flakes in a mortar. Reserve ½ teaspoon and set aside.

In a small saucepan bring the Chicken Stock and Golden Mountain sauce to a boil over high heat. Add the beef and cook until the meat is heated and liquid is absorbed. The beef should be medium done. Quickly remove the pan from the heat. Add the ground peppers and lime juice and mix. Add the toasted rice, green onions, mint leaves, coriander, and fish sauce in order, and mix thoroughly.

Serve immediately on a bed of lettuce as in the Prawn Salad (page 65).

Serves 2.

BEEF SALAD III
(Salad Nuar San)

This alternative to Yum Yai and Yum Nuar uses the same cut of beef, but the meat is marinated and pan-fried instead of charcoal-grilled. The salad is extremely garlicky and sour. In this dish, the jalapeño chili peppers are optional.

> 1 tablespoon Golden Mountain sauce
> 2 tablespoons oyster sauce
> 1 tablespoon palm sugar
> 1 teaspoon ground white pepper
> 1 head garlic, minced (approximately 2 ounces)
> 10-ounce center section of chuck roast, cut along the membrane holding the sections together
> 3 tablespoons oil
> 5 ounces fresh pickling cucumber
> 1 to 2 boiling onions (approximately 4 ounces)
> 4 tablespoons fresh lime juice
> 2 tablespoons fish sauce
> 2 to 3 red jalapeño or serrano chili peppers, sliced into rings (optional)
> 2 to 3 small tomatoes, sliced ¼ inch thick (5 to 8 ounces)
> 2 green onions, sliced into 2-inch lengths
> Red lettuce, washed and drained
> Leaves from 3 sprigs fresh coriander

To prepare the marinade, combine the Golden Mountain Sauce, oyster sauce, palm sugar, white pepper, and garlic in a bowl large enough to hold the beef.

Cut the section of chuck roast in half, trim any fat, and add it to the marinade, coating it completely. Refrigerate for 30 minutes or longer, until most of the liquid has been absorbed.

Heat a well-seasoned pan over medium-low heat. Add oil and pan-fry the beef for about 6 minutes on each of the four sides until it is medium-well done. After 10 minutes of cooking, add any remaining marinade to the pan. If it starts to burn, reduce the heat.

Slice the cucumbers in half lengthwise. Slice each section into ⅛-inch pieces and set aside. Peel the boiling onion and slice into ⅛-inch rings. Separate the rings and set aside.

When the beef is done, allow it to cool slightly. Slice it across the grain
into pieces ⅛ inch thick and place in a medium bowl. Skim the fat
from the pan drippings and add the drippings to the bowl. Add the
lime juice, fish sauce, and peppers. Thoroughly mix so that the beef
can absorb some of the liquid. Add the cucumber and onions and
mix. Add the tomatoes and green onions, and mix lightly so that
the tomatoes remain in whole pieces.
Garnish with coriander and serve immediately on a bed of red lettuce.

Serves 4.

SARDINE SALAD
(Yum Bla Gra Bong)

Sardine salad is very easy to make. Kwan's mother created this
recipe and served it often, since it is very economical as well as tasty.
She liked to serve it hot, but you can reduce the amount of jalapeño chili
peppers according to your taste. It is "tomato-y" and minty, but not as
fishy as you might expect.

> 15-ounce can sardines in tomato sauce
> 4 tablespoons fresh lime juice
> 1 large stalk lemon grass, thinly sliced
> 2 medium shallots, peeled and sliced ¹⁄₁₆ inch thick (approxi-
>   mately 2 ounces)
> Leaves from 4 whole coriander plants, lightly chopped
> 2 tablespoons fish sauce
> 2 green onions, thinly sliced
> 20 Thai or Italian basil leaves
> 5 jalapeño or serrano chili peppers, thinly sliced
> 30 to 40 medium mint leaves
> Red lettuce, washed and drained

Heat the sardines in their tomato sauce in a small saucepan over low
heat for about 4 minutes. Turn and cook another 3 minutes to heat
evenly.
In a medium bowl combine the sardines and lime juice, breaking the
sardines into smaller pieces. Add the lemon grass, shallots, corian-

der, fish sauce, green onions, basil leaves, chili peppers, and mint leaves. Mix well.

Arrange on a bed of red lettuce and serve immediately.

Serves 4.

 ## BEAN THREAD SALAD
(Yum Woon Sen)

This salad literally "slithers" down your throat. It is very easy to make, and combines the sour, sweet, and salty flavors so delectable in Thai cuisine.

¼ cup large dried shrimp (approximately ½ ounce)
2 ounces mung bean thread
4 to 5 raw medium prawns, shelled and deveined (3 to 4 ounces)
3 tablespoons fresh lime juice
2½ tablespoons fish sauce
¾ teaspoon sugar
1 to 2 medium button mushroom, thinly sliced
1 stalk celery, thinly sliced at an angle
1 green onion, sliced into 1½-inch lengths
1 tablespoon coarsely chopped coriander leaves
Red lettuce, washed and drained

Pound the dried shrimp in a mortar to flatten them into soft, crumbly pieces. Set aside. (They should still be in relatively whole pieces.)

In a medium bowl soak the mung bean thread in water for 1 hour until soft. Using a strainer to hold the noodles, dip them in boiling water for 1 second. Remove and immediately dip into ice water to stop the cooking. Drain well and set aside.

Using a strainer to hold the prawns, parboil for 6 seconds until they turn pink. Drain well.

In a medium bowl combine the prawns and lime juice; allow to stand for 1 minute. Add the dried shrimp, mung bean thread, fish sauce, sugar, mushroom, celery, green onion, and coriander leaves.

Arrange the salad on a bed of lettuce and serve immediately.

Serves 4.

CHILI PEPPER SALAD
(Yum Prik Yuak Gung Hang)

This particular recipe comes with a warning. Chili Pepper Salad looks very appetizing and alluring, but don't try it unless you can take the heat! Despite its hotness, you can still taste its piquant, aromatic flavor. In Thailand it is served without the lettuce along with other entrees and is eaten with rice, which helps to cool the palate.

½ cup large dried shrimp
3 medium shallots (approximately 3½ ounces)
5 Thai or jalapeño chili peppers
½ medium tomato (approximately 3½ ounces)
1 tablespoon fish sauce
2 tablespoons fresh lime juice
½ teaspoon sugar
Iceberg or romaine lettuce, washed and drained

Pound the dried shrimp in a mortar to flatten and soften. Set aside. Don't use a blender for this step because you want to be able to see whole shrimp in the salad.

Leaving skins intact, charcoal-grill the shallots, chili peppers, and tomato over high heat. Grill until the skins become charred, turning occasionally until each is soft. Remove from the grill. (Cook the tomato just half-way. If overcooked, it will become soggy and won't hold up in the salad.)

Peel and discard the charred skins, leaving a little to retain the charcoal smell and flavor.

Remove the stems from the chili peppers and thinly slice lengthwise, saving the seeds. Thinly slice the shallots. Cut the tomato into ½-inch cubes.

Combine the chili peppers, shallots, tomato, shrimp, fish sauce, lime juice, and sugar in a medium bowl.

Serve on a bed of lettuce as in the Prawn Salad (page 65).

Serves 4.

FRESH MIXED VEGETABLES WITH

SPICY PEANUT DRESSING
(Salad Nam Kon)

Spicy Peanut Dressing looks very much like a Thousand Island Dressing, but that is where the similarity ends. A better name for it would be Spicy Garlic Dressing. Pour the dressing over vegetables or use it as a dipping sauce.

Spicy Peanut Dressing
>3 large heads pickled garlic
>1 tablespoon raw peanuts
>5 tablespoons oil
>2 teaspoons minced garlic
>4 hard-boiled egg yolks
>2½ tablespoons sugar
>1 teaspoon salt
>5 tablespoons vinegar
>1 tablespoon brine from pickled garlic

Discard the outer skins, stems, and bases of the pickled garlic. Thinly slice the heads and place in blender.

Dry-roast the raw peanuts in a skillet for about 10 minutes over medium-low heat, until brown. Turn frequently, being careful not to let them burn. Add to the blender.

Heat a well-seasoned pan over medium-high heat and add the oil. When oil is hot, add the minced garlic. Stir-fry until brown and crisp, being careful not to let it burn.

Add the browned garlic and 1 teaspoon of the frying oil to the blender along with the hard-boiled egg yolks, sugar, salt, vinegar, and brine from the pickled garlic. Blend until the mixture becomes thick and creamy. Serve in a separate bowl.

>Makes about 1½ cups.

Mixed vegetables
>Oil for deep-frying
>2½ ounces firm tofu, ¾ by 1¼ by 3 inches
>½ head iceberg lettuce, washed and drained
>1 cucumber, peeled and sliced
>1 medium tomato, sliced
>3½ ounces bean sprouts

In a deep-fryer, heat the oil to 450°. Deep-fry the tofu for 3 minutes, until golden brown and crisp. Drain on paper towels. Cool and slice into pieces ¼ inch thick. Set aside.

Arrange the lettuce, cucumbers, tomatoes, and bean sprouts in a shallow bowl. Garnish with the fried tofu; serve with the dressing.

Serves 4.

GREEN PAPAYA SALAD
(Som Tham Mara Gor)

Green Papaya Salad originated in the northeastern part of Thailand, but it is now common in the marketplaces of Bangkok. Green papaya is difficult to obtain in the United States; however, carrots may be substituted with little loss of flavor. In this recipe use a mortar and pestle to crush and bruise the papaya and green beans in order to release their essence and allow them to absorb the flavors better. This crunchy salad has a medium-hot dressing and is served with steamed sweet rice in Thailand. For a more colorful salad, substitute 2 tablespoons of shredded carrots for an equal amount of green papaya.

> 2 teaspoons raw peanuts (optional)
> 2 medium cloves garlic
> 2 to 4 fresh or frozen Thai chili peppers
> ½ cup large dried shrimp (approximately 1½ ounces)
> ½ cup green beans, cut into 1½-inch lengths (approximately 2 ounces)
> 2 cups shredded green papaya, peeled and seeded, or shredded carrots (approximately 8 ounces)
> 4 large cherry tomatoes, quartered (approximately 5 ounces)
> 1 teaspoon palm sugar
> 8 teaspoons fresh lime juice
> 6 teaspoons fish sauce
> Iceberg or romaine lettuce, washed and drained

Dry-roast the raw peanuts in a skillet for about 10 minutes over medium-low heat until brown, flipping frequently. Be careful not to let them burn. In a mortar, pound the peanuts into small pieces. Remove from the mortar and set aside.

Place the garlic and Thai chili peppers in a clean mortar. Pound into tiny pieces. Add the dried shrimp and pound until flattened into soft, crumbly pieces. Gradually add the green beans and green papaya. Pound to slightly crush and soften. Add the cherry tomatoes and palm sugar; lightly pound to release some of the tomato's juices and to dissolve the sugar.

In a medium bowl combine the crushed ingredients, lime juice, fish sauce, and ground peanuts.

Serve on a bed of lettuce.

Serves 4.

 ### DRIED SHRIMP AND SALTY LETTUCE SALAD (Pat Gat Dong)

This salad is actually salty and sweet, with hotness from Thai chili peppers and ginger. If it's too hot for your taste, reduce the amount of chilies and ginger next time you make it. When Kwan makes this for herself she adds more chili peppers and lime juice, but for the cookbook it's been toned down. Dried Shrimp and Salty Lettuce Salad is eaten with rice soup or steamed rice and is great for breakfast or lunch. It is easy to prepare.

> 5-ounce can salted lettuce, with its brine
> 1-inch piece fresh ginger, peeled and sliced into fine julienne
>   pieces (approximately ¾ ounce)
> 20 large dried shrimp (approximately 2 ounces)
> 1 large clove garlic, thinly sliced
> 1 Thai chili pepper or jalapeño chili pepper, thinly sliced
> 3 tablespoons fresh lime juice
> ½ teaspoon sugar
> Iceberg or romaine lettuce, washed and drained (optional)

Slice the salted lettuce into pieces 1 inch long.

Combine the salted lettuce, brine, ginger, dried shrimp, garlic, chili pepper, lime juice, and sugar in a medium bowl.

Serve on a bed of lettuce.

Serves 4.

CUCUMBER SALAD
(Ajaat)

This recipe is called a salad but it is used as a dipping sauce for Shrimp and Ground Pork Toast (page 39), Beef Satay (page 41), and Yellow Curry Chicken (page 116). It is easy to make, and is best served fresh.

10 thin slices cucumber
4 to 5 thin slices red onion
3 to 4 round slices jalapeño chili pepper
¼ cup Kwan's Sweet and Sour Sauce (page 87)
Leaves from 5 sprigs fresh coriander

Layer the cucumber, red onion, and chili pepper in a small serving bowl. Add the sweet and sour sauce. Garnish with the coriander leaves and serve.

SAUTÉED RADISH
(Yum Hua Chai Bo)

Since the Sautéed Radish is quite sweet and salty, it is typically eaten in the morning for breakfast with rice soup, which is very bland. To heighten the smell and flavor of the radish it is cooked until it is transformed into shiny, dark brown shreds. The eggs should be mixed throughout while still adhering to the radish.

4 tablespoons oil
1 tablespoon minced garlic
7-ounce package salted radish, shredded
3 tablespoons sugar
2 to 3 large eggs

Heat a well-seasoned pan over medium-high heat and add the oil. When the oil is hot, add the garlic and sauté until lightly browned.
Add the salted radish and sugar. Stir-fry for 30 seconds to heat thoroughly. Flatten the radish and break the eggs over the surface. Smash the eggs into the surface, breaking the yokes, and spread with a spatula. Without stirring, cook for 30 seconds to allow the eggs to set slightly. Flip the radish once and, without stirring, allow

to cook for another minute. Break into pieces and cook another 4 to 5 minutes until the radish turns shiny and dark brown, flipping occasionally. Be careful not to let the mixture burn; lower the heat, if necessary. Serve immediately.

Serves 4.

SAUTÉED VEGETABLES
(Pat Tua Kaek)

At Siam Cuisine this recipe is used to cook various types of vegetables. The recipe here uses green beans but suggests several alternatives. The seasoning is mild and will complement any Thai meal. Sautéed green beans are very easy to prepare and can be cooked at the last minute. Blanch the beans first to eliminate their raw smell without having to overcook them. For best results this dish should be cooked over very high heat.

> 16 ounces Blue Lake green beans, cut into 2-inch lengths *or*
> 16 ounces sliced cabbage *or*
> 16 ounces broccoli
> 2 tablespoons oil
> 1 teaspoon minced garlic
> 1 teaspoon bean sauce
> 1 tablespoon oyster sauce
> 1 tablespoon Golden Mountain sauce
> 1 teaspoon sugar

Blanch the green beans in boiling water for 10 seconds. Drain and set aside.
Heat a well-seasoned pan over high heat and add the oil. When the oil is hot, add the garlic and bean sauce. Sauté until the garlic is browned.
Add the green beans and stir-fry for 1 minute, flipping occasionally. Add the oyster sauce, Golden Mountain sauce, and sugar. Stir-fry for 3 minutes more until the green beans are tender but still crunchy.

Serves 4.

To prepare this recipe with broccoli, cut the flowers 2½ inches from the top and separate into smaller sections. Peel the stems and cut into rectangular pieces about 3 by 1¼ by ³⁄₁₆ inches. Cook the broccoli or sliced cabbage as you would the green beans.

Curry Pastes and Sauces

 BASIC CURRY PASTE
(Kruang Gang Tua Bai)

Basic Curry Paste is used in such recipes as Fish Cakes (page 40), Fish Curry with Somen Noodles (page 162), Red Curry Fish (page 144), Peanut Curry Sauce (page 92), and Panang Beef (page 106). For best flavor and aroma, we suggest roasting the dried spices before grinding; however, this step is not necessary for the successful completion of the recipes. To get a smooth paste, slice the various ingredients as thinly as possible to help break up the fiber. The curry paste can be stored in the refrigerator for 3 to 4 weeks in a sealed jar, or in the freezer for up to 3 months.

> 1½ tablespoons thinly sliced fresh or frozen galanga, firmly packed *or* 2 to 3 pieces dried
> 6 to 8 pieces dried Kaffir lime rind
> ⅛ teaspoon cumin seed
> ¼ teaspoon coriander seed
> ¼ teaspoon black peppercorns
> 1½ tablespoons thinly sliced fresh lemon grass, firmly packed
> ½ cup thinly sliced garlic, firmly packed
> 2½ to 3 tablespoons thinly sliced shallots, firmly packed
> ½ teaspoon shrimp paste
> ½ teaspoon salt
> ½ cup water (optional—use only if processing in a blender)

If dried galanga is used, soak it for 1 to 2 hours in hot water. Drain and slice thinly. Reserve 1 tablespoon, firmly packed.

Soak the Kaffir lime rind for 1 to 2 hours in hot water. Scrape off and discard the white pulp that lines it. Slice thinly and reserve 1 teaspoon, firmly packed.

Dry-roast the cumin seeds, coriander seeds, and black peppercorns in a skillet over medium-high heat for 4 to 5 minutes, until you begin to smell them. Flip frequently to prevent burning. Place in a spice grinder or mortar and grind or pound to a powder.

Place the powdered spices, galanga, Kaffir lime rind, lemon grass, garlic, shallots, shrimp paste, and salt in a mortar or blender; pound or grind to a fine, smooth paste. (If using a blender, add the water to process.)

Makes about 1¼ cups.

 ## GREEN CURRY PASTE
(Kruang Gang Keow Wan)

Green Curry Paste is the hottest of the curry pastes but, depending on your own tolerance, the number of Thai chili peppers can be adjusted. The chili peppers are very aromatic, providing flavor as well as the ominous green color of the curry. This recipe also calls for fresh coriander to supplement the color without adding bulk, which would decrease the potency and flavor of the chili peppers. Green Curry Paste can be stored in the refrigerator for 3 to 4 weeks in a sealed jar or in the freezer for up to 3 months. We recommend using a blender to complete this recipe.

> 1½ tablespoons thinly sliced fresh or frozen galanga, firmly packed *or* 2 to 3 pieces dried
> 6 to 8 pieces dried Kaffir lime rind
> ¼ teaspoon cumin seed
> ½ teaspoon coriander seed
> ¼ teaspoon black peppercorns
> 1 bunch fresh coriander, roots removed
> ½ cup cold water
> 5½ teaspoons thinly sliced fresh lemon grass, firmly packed
> ½ cup thinly sliced garlic, firmly packed
> 2½ to 3 tablespoons thinly sliced shallots, firmly packed
> ½ teaspoon salt
> ½ teaspoon shrimp paste
> 25 fresh or frozen Thai chili peppers, stems removed
> 1 teaspoon chopped coriander roots, firmly packed

If dried galanga is used, soak it for 1 to 2 hours in hot water. Drain and slice thinly. Reserve 1 tablespoon, firmly packed.

Soak the Kaffir lime rind for 1 to 2 hours in hot water. Scrape off and discard the white pulp that lines it. Slice thinly and reserve 1 teaspoon, firmly packed.

Dry-roast the cumin seeds, coriander seeds, and black peppercorns in a skillet over medium-high heat for 4 to 5 minutes, until you begin to smell them. Flip frequently to prevent burning. Place in a spice grinder or mortar and grind or pound to a powder. Set aside.

Place the fresh coriander and cold water in a blender and grind into a paste. Using a fine strainer, squeeze out and save all the green liquid, discarding the pulp. Pour the liquid back into the blender.

Add the galanga, Kaffir lime rind, powdered spices, lemon grass, garlic, shallots, salt, shrimp paste, chili peppers, and coriander roots to the blender. Grind to a fine, smooth paste.

Makes about 2 cups.

RED CURRY PASTE I
(Nam Prik Gang Paet)

Red Curry Paste I is used to make Red Curry Chicken. The paste itself is very hot and pungent, but cooking it in coconut milk tones it down. The paste can be stored in the refrigerator for 3 to 4 weeks or in the freezer for 3 months.

5¼ teaspoons thinly sliced fresh or frozen galanga, firmly packed *or* 3 to 4 pieces dried

6 to 8 pieces dried Kaffir lime rind

22 to 30 dried red chili peppers, 2 to 3 inches long, or dried Cayenne peppers

1 dried New Mexico chili pepper, stem removed

¼ teaspoon cumin seed

½ teaspoon coriander seed

¼ teaspoon black peppercorns

5½ teaspoons thinly sliced fresh lemon grass, firmly packed

½ cup thinly sliced garlic, firmly packed

2½ to 3 tablespoons thinly sliced shallots, firmly packed

½ teaspoon shrimp paste

½ teaspoon salt

½ cup water (optional—use only if processing in a blender)

If dried galanga is used, soak it for 1 to 2 hours in hot water. Drain and thinly slice. Reserve 1 tablespoon, firmly packed.

Soak the Kaffir lime rind for 1 to 2 hours in hot water. Scrape off and
    discard the white pulp that lines it. Slice thinly and reserve 1 tea-
    spoon, firmly packed.
Soak the chili peppers in warm water for about 15 minutes, until soft.
    Remove and discard the seeds and set the chilies aside.
Dry-roast the cumin seeds, coriander seeds, and black peppercorns in a
    skillet over medium-high heat for 4 to 5 minutes, until you begin to
    smell them. Flip frequently to prevent burning. Place in a spice
    grinder or mortar and grind or pound to a powder. Set aside.
Place the galanga, Kaffir lime rind, chili peppers, powdered spices,
    lemon grass, garlic, shallots, shrimp paste, and salt in a mortar or
    blender. Pound or grind the ingredients to a fine, smooth paste. (If
    using a blender, add the water to process.)

Makes about 1¼ cups.

RED CURRY PASTE II
(Kruang Gang Pla Rat Prik / Mu Pat Prik King)

This recipe, which is used in Pork and Green Beans in Red
Curry Paste (page 99) and in Fried Fish with Spicy Sauce (page 134), is
not as hot and spicy as Red Curry Paste I. It can be stored in the
refrigerator for up to 3 weeks or in the freezer for 3 months.

2 tablespoons thinly sliced fresh or frozen galanga, firmly
    packed or 3 to 4 pieces dried
2 to 3 pieces dried Kaffir lime rind
7 dried red chili peppers, 2 to 3 inches long, or dried Cayenne
    peppers
1 dried New Mexico chili pepper, stem removed
½ cup thinly sliced fresh lemon grass, firmly packed
¼ cup thinly sliced shallots, firmly packed
2 tablespoons thinly sliced garlic, firmly packed
½ cup water (optional—use only if processing in a blender)

If dried galanga is used, soak it for 1 to 2 hours in hot water. Drain and
    slice thinly. Reserve 4 teaspoons, firmly packed.
Soak the Kaffir lime rind for 1 to 2 hours in hot water. Scrape off and
    discard the white pulp that lines it. Slice thinly, and reserve ¼ tea-
    spoon, firmly packed.

Soak the chili peppers in warm water for about 15 minutes, until soft.
Remove and discard the seeds and set the chilies aside.
Place the galanga, Kaffir lime rind, chili peppers, lemon grass, shallots,
and garlic in a mortar or blender. Pound or grind the ingredients to
a fine, smooth paste. (If using a blender, add the water to process.)

Makes about 1 cup.

 ## RED CURRY PASTE III
(Kruang Gang Haw Mok)

Traditionally Red Curry Paste III is ground in a mortar, resulting
in a very dry paste, which is necessary for the successful completion of
Steamed Fish Curry in Banana Leaf Bowl (page 146). The grinding will
take an experienced cook anywhere from 30 minutes to an hour to complete; we therefore recommend using a blender. Be sure not to leave any
large pieces in the paste; they will taste bitter. This paste can be stored
in the refrigerator for 3 to 4 weeks or in the freezer for 3 months.

> ¼ cup thinly sliced fresh or frozen galanga, firmly packed or 5
>   to 7 pieces dried
> 6 to 8 pieces dried Kaffir lime rind
> 48 dried red chili peppers, 2 to 3 inches long, or dried Cayenne
>   peppers (approximately 2 ounces)
> 1 dried New Mexico or California chili pepper
> 3½ to 4½ teaspoons salt
> ½ cup thinly sliced fresh lemon grass, firmly packed
> ¾ cup thinly sliced shallots, firmly packed
> ¼ cup thinly sliced garlic, firmly packed
> ½ to 1½ cups water (optional—use only if processing in a
>   blender)

If dried galanga is used, soak it for 1 to 2 hours in hot water. Drain and
slice thinly. Reserve 2 tablespoons plus 2 teaspoons, firmly packed.
Soak the Kaffir lime rind for 1 to 2 hours in hot water. Scrape off and
discard the white pulp that lines it. Slice thinly, and reserve 1 teaspoon, firmly packed.
Soak the chili peppers in warm water for about 15 minutes, until soft.
Remove and discard the seeds and set the chilies aside.

Place the galanga, Kaffir lime rind, chili peppers, salt, lemon grass, shallots, and garlic in a mortar or blender. Pound or grind the ingredients to a fine, smooth paste. (If using a blender, add water as needed to process.)

Makes about 2 cups.

 RED CURRY PASTE IV
(Gang Kua Sapparot Gap Gung)

Red Curry Paste IV is a hot, pungent, dark orange mixture used for making Pineapple Curry (page 147). Like the other curry pastes, it can be stored in the refrigerator for 3 to 4 weeks or in the freezer for 3 months.

> 1½ tablespoons thinly sliced fresh or frozen galanga, firmly packed *or* 2 to 3 pieces dried
> 6 to 8 pieces dried Kaffir lime rind
> 1½ tablespoons thinly sliced fresh lemon grass, firmly packed
> 3 tablespoons thinly sliced shallots, firmly packed
> ½ cup thinly sliced garlic, firmly packed
> 2 tablespoons dried shrimp (approximately ½ ounce)
> 12 dried red chili peppers, 2 to 3 inches long, or dried Cayenne peppers
> 1 dried New Mexico or California chili pepper, stem removed, torn into several pieces
> ½ cup water (optional—use only if processing in a blender)

If dried galanga is used, soak it for 1 to 2 hours in hot water. Drain and slice thinly. Reserve 1 tablespoon, firmly packed.

Soak the Kaffir lime rind for 1 to 2 hours in hot water. Scrape off and discard the white pulp that lines it. Slice thinly, and reserve 1 teaspoon, firmly packed.

Place the galanga, Kaffir lime rind, lemon grass, shallots, garlic, dried shrimp, and chili peppers in a mortar or blender. Pound or grind to a fine, smooth paste. (If using a blender, add ½ cup water to process.)

Makes about 1 cup.

YELLOW CURRY PASTE
(Kruang Gang Garee)

This curry paste is Muslim in origin and is used for Yellow Curry Chicken (page 116). It is hot to the taste, but loses much of its strength when cooked with coconut milk. It can be stored in the refrigerator for 3 to 4 weeks or in the freezer for 3 months.

>   1½ tablespoons thinly sliced fresh or frozen galanga, firmly packed *or* 2 to 3 pieces dried
>   6 to 8 pieces dried Kaffir lime rind
>   7 to 8 dried red chili peppers, 2 to 3 inches long, or dried Cayenne peppers
>   ⅛ teaspoon cumin seed
>   ¼ teaspoon coriander seed
>   ¼ teaspoon black peppercorns
>   1½ tablespoons thinly sliced fresh lemon grass, firmly packed
>   ½ cup thinly sliced garlic, firmly packed
>   2½ to 3 tablespoons thinly sliced shallots, firmly packed
>   1 tablespoon yellow curry powder
>   ½ teaspoon shrimp paste
>   ½ teaspoon salt
>   ½ cup water (optional—use only if processing in a blender)

If dried galanga is used, soak it for 1 to 2 hours in hot water. Drain and slice thinly. Reserve 1 tablespoon, firmly packed.

Soak the Kaffir lime rind for 1 to 2 hours in hot water. Scrape off and discard the white pulp that lines it. Slice thinly, and reserve 1 teaspoon, firmly packed.

Soak the chili peppers in warm water for about 15 minutes, until soft. Remove and discard the seeds and set the chilies aside.

Dry-roast the cumin seeds, coriander seeds, and black peppercorns in a skillet over medium-high heat for 4 to 5 minutes, until you begin to smell them. Flip frequently to prevent burning. Place in a spice grinder or mortar and grind or pound to a powder. Set aside.

Place the galanga, Kaffir lime rind, chili peppers, powdered spices, lemon grass, garlic, shallots, yellow curry powder, shrimp paste, and salt in a mortar or blender. Pound or grind the ingredients to a fine, smooth paste. (If using a blender, add ½ cup water to process.)

Makes about 1¼ cups.

MUSUMAN CURRY PASTE
(Kruang Gang Musuman)

Musuman Curry Paste is used in a Muslim curry. (It is interesting to note that "mussulman," which sounds like "musuman," is an archaic word referring to a Muslim.) It incorporates several ingredients which are quite different from the other curries given in this book. We recommend you use freshly ground whole cloves and cardamom seeds to heighten the smell and flavor. It can be kept in the refrigerator for up to 2 weeks in a sealed container or in the freezer for 2 months.

> 1½ tablespoons thinly sliced fresh or frozen galanga, firmly packed, or 2 to 3 pieces dried
> 3 teaspoons coriander seed
> 2 teaspoons cumin seed
> 1 dried New Mexico chili pepper, stem and seeds removed, torn into several pieces
> 14 dried red chili peppers, 2 to 3 inches long, or dried Cayenne peppers, seeds removed
> ½ cup chopped garlic
> ½ cup chopped shallots
> ½ cup thinly sliced fresh lemon grass, firmly packed
> 1 teaspoon oil (optional—use if necessary to prevent sticking)
> ½ cup water (optional—use only if processing in a blender)
> 1 teaspoon freshly ground cloves
> 1 teaspoon ground cinnamon
> ½ teaspoon freshly ground cardamom seed
> 1 teaspoon salt
> ¼ teaspoon shrimp paste

If dried galanga is used, soak it for 1 to 2 hours in hot water. Drain and slice thinly. Reserve 1 tablespoon, firmly packed.

Dry-roast the coriander seeds, cumin seeds, chili peppers, garlic, shallots, ¼ cup of the lemon grass, and ½ tablespoon of the galanga in a well-seasoned pan at medium heat. If it starts to stick, add 1 teaspoon oil. Roast until the chili peppers turn dark red and you can smell them. Be careful not to let the mixture burn.

Place the roasted ingredients in a mortar or blender and pound or grind to a fine, smooth paste. (If using a blender, add ½ cup water to process.)

Add the cloves, cinnamon, cardamom, salt, and shrimp paste and the rest of the lemon grass and galanga to the mortar or blender. Continue pounding or grinding to a fine, smooth paste.

Makes about 2 cups.

GREEN CHILI SAUCE
(Nam Jim Keow)

Green Chili Sauce was created by Kwan's family in Thailand and cannot be found in the restaurants there. It is a wonderfully tangy, sour, sweet dipping sauce. Depending on the potency of your chili peppers, it can be very hot. It adds a zesty contrast to many seafood dishes and greatly enhances their flavor. At the restaurant, it is served with Filet of Fish Clay Pot (page 153), Mussel Clay Pot (page 152), Fresh Baked Fish in Banana Leaf (page 136), and the various Charcoal-Broiled Seafood dishes (pages 44–46). The sauce can be kept in the refrigerator for 3 to 4 months. Stir before using.

> ½ bunch fresh coriander (approximately 1½ ounces), roots removed
> 3 to 4 jalapeño or serrano chili peppers, stems removed
> ¼ cup chopped garlic
> ¼ cup sugar
> 1⅛ teaspoons salt
> 1 cup white vinegar

Place the coriander, chili peppers, garlic, sugar, salt, and white vinegar in a blender. Grind until all ingredients are completely liquefied.

Makes about 2 cups.

KWAN'S SWEET AND SOUR SAUCE
(Nam Breow Waan Kwan)

Kwan's Sweet and Sour Sauce is an all-purpose sauce that is used as a base for other sauces. In these recipes it is also added to some of the stir-fry dishes to make the flavors come alive. Always keep some on hand in the refrigerator; it will keep for about 6 months in a sealed jar.

1 cup sugar
2 teaspoons salt
¾ cup white vinegar

Combine the sugar, salt, and vinegar in a small saucepan. Heat over
   medium heat until all ingredients are dissolved, stirring occasionally.

Makes 1½ cups.

PEANUT AND CUCUMBER SAUCE
(Nam Jim Bla Tot Man)

Peanut and Cucumber Sauce is served with Fish Cakes (page
40) and Angel Wings (page 119). For better smell and flavor, grind the
peanuts just before making the sauce.

2 teaspoons raw peanuts
7 to 8 thin slices cucumber
¼ teaspoon red chili sauce, or to taste
¼ cup Kwan's Sweet and Sour Sauce (page 87)
Leaves from 3 sprigs fresh coriander

Dry-roast the peanuts in a skillet for 10 minutes over medium-low heat
   until evenly browned, flipping frequently. Cool to room temperature. In a mortar pound the peanuts into small pieces. Set aside.
Layer the cucumber slices and red chili sauce in a small serving bowl.
   Add the sweet and sour sauce. Garnish with the ground peanuts
   and coriander leaves.

Makes approximately ¼ cup.

SPICY PEANUT SAUCE
(Nam Jim Tofu Tot)

Serve this dipping sauce with Fried Tofu (page 39) or Fried
Sweet Potatoes (page 43).

2 teaspoons raw peanuts
⅙ teaspoon red chili sauce, or to taste
¼ cup Kwan's Sweet and Sour Sauce (page 87)
Leaves from 2 sprigs fresh coriander

Dry-roast the peanuts in a skillet for 10 minutes over medium-low heat, until evenly browned, flipping frequently. Cool to room temperature. In a mortar pound peanuts into small pieces. Set aside.

Combine the red chili sauce and sweet and sour sauce in a small serving bowl. Garnish with the ground peanuts and coriander leaves.

Makes approximately ¼ cup.

THAI BARBECUED CHICKEN SAUCE
(Nam Jim Gai Yang)

This sauce goes well with Barbecued Chicken (page 122), Fresh Baked Fish in Banana Leaf (page 136), Garlic Mackerel (page 142), Grilled Garlic Quail (page 123), and Jumbo Prawns (page 141).

> ¼ cup Kwan's Sweet and Sour Sauce (page 87)
> ¼ teaspoon red chili sauce, or to taste
> 1 teaspoon fish sauce
> Leaves from 1 sprig fresh coriander

Combine sweet and sour sauce, red chili sauce, and fish sauce in a small serving bowl. Garnish with coriander leaves.

Makes approximately ¼ cup.

SPICY CHILI OIL
(Nam Prik Paow)

I always like to have Spicy Chili Oil available. It can be sautéed with various types of seafood for a quick meal, adding a sweet, pungent flavor, and is also an ingredient in the recipes for Peanut Curry Sauce (page 92) and Musuman Curry (page 107). It is a medium-hot sauce, getting its deep red color from New Mexico chili peppers. It can be stored in the refrigerator for 2 to 3 months; bring back to room temperature and stir in the oil before using.

> 3 ounces preserved tamarind
> ¾ cup hot water
> ⅓ cup dried shrimp
> 1 cup oil
> ⅓ cup thinly sliced garlic

1 cup thinly sliced shallots

10 dried red chili peppers, 2 to 3 inches long, or dried Cayenne
   peppers

5 dried New Mexico chili peppers, stems and seeds removed,
   torn into 2-inch pieces

½ cup water

½ cup sugar

5 tablespoons plus 2 teaspoons fish sauce

⅓ cup creamy peanut butter

In a small bowl, soak the tamarind in the hot water for 30 minutes, until soft. Work the tamarind with your hands for 10 minutes to release the pulp. Press pulp through a strainer. Squeeze out all the liquid and pulp and discard the twigs and seeds. Reserve ½ cup and set aside.

Place the dried shrimp in a blender and grind into very fine pieces. Reserve ⅓ cup and set aside.

Heat a well-seasoned pan or wok over medium-high heat and add the oil. When the oil is hot, add the garlic. Sauté until transparent. Remove the garlic and place in a blender.

Using the same oil, sauté the shallots until transparent. Remove and add to the blender.

Reduce the heat to medium low and add the chili peppers to the oil. Sauté until tender, being careful not to let them burn. Turn off the heat and add the peppers to the blender. Discard any seeds that remain in the oil; they are burnt and will make the Spicy Chili Oil taste bitter. Set the oil aside.

Add the water to the blender and grind the ingredients to a fine paste. Pour the paste back into the oil and add the dried shrimp, tamarind, sugar, fish sauce, and peanut butter. Reduce over medium-high heat for 20 to 30 minutes, until the mixture becomes thick and grainy and a thin layer of oil appears on the surface. Stir constantly to prevent sticking or burning.

Makes approximately 2 cups.

SPICY CHILI OIL FOR
 ## HOT AND SOUR PRAWN SOUP
(Nam Prik Paow Thom Yum)

This sauce is made especially for Hot and Sour Prawn Soup (page 54) and for Seafood Clay Pot (page 151). It is cooked in a manner similar to Spicy Chili Oil, but the resulting sauce is smoother and glossier, without the surface oil. Stored in a tightly sealed jar in the refrigerator, it will keep for 2 to 3 months.

> 3 ounces preserved tamarind
> ¾ cup hot water
> ¼ cup oil
> ⅓ cup thinly sliced garlic
> 1 cup thinly sliced shallots
> 10 dried red chili peppers, 2 to 3 inches long, or dried Cayenne chili peppers
> 5 dried New Mexico chili peppers, stems and seeds removed, torn into 2-inch pieces
> ½ cup water
> ½ cup sugar
> 5 tablespoons plus 2 teaspoons fish sauce

In a small bowl soak the tamarind in ¾ cup hot water for 30 minutes, until soft. Work the tamarind with your hands for 10 minutes to release the pulp. Press the pulp through a strainer. Squeeze out all the liquid and pulp and discard the twigs and seeds. Reserve ½ cup and set aside.

Heat a well-seasoned pan or wok over medium-high heat and add the oil. When the oil is hot, add the garlic. Sauté until transparent. Remove the garlic and place in a blender.

Using the same oil, sauté the shallots until transparent. Remove and add to the blender.

Reduce the heat to medium low and add the chili peppers to the oil. Sauté until tender, being careful not to let them burn. Turn off the heat and add the peppers to the blender. Discard any seeds that remain in the oil; they are burnt and will make the Spicy Chili Oil taste bitter. Set the oil aside.

Add ½ cup water to the blender and grind the ingredients to a fine paste. Pour the paste back into the oil and add the tamarind, sugar, and fish sauce. Reduce over medium heat for 20 to 30 minutes, until the surface becomes glossy. Stir only to prevent the paste from sticking or burning. Do not overcook. The mixture will caramelize and become hard when cooled.

Makes approximately 2 cups.

PEANUT CURRY SAUCE
(Nam Jim Satay)

Peanut Curry Sauce is a taste sensation, and a wonderful complement to Beef Satay (page 41). It is a thick, creamy, medium-hot sauce. It can be prepared in advance and frozen for 4 to 5 months in meal-sized servings, if properly sealed. If the aroma is gone after defrosting, add a pinch of cinnamon and stir well to bring back the original freshness. When reducing the sauce, never allow more than 1 tablespoon of oil to be released to the surface, or it will give the Beef Satay an oily taste.

¼ cup Basic Curry Paste (page 79)
2 tablespoons Spicy Chili Oil (page 89)
1 tablespoon ground cayenne pepper
1 tablespoon paprika (for color)
¾ teaspoon ground cinnamon
⅛ teaspoon ground cumin
⅛ teaspoon ground cloves
¼ cup plus 2 tablespoons sugar
5¼ cups thick coconut milk
¼ cup fish sauce
⅔ cup fresh Chicken Stock (page 53)
2 tablespoons creamy peanut butter

Combine the curry paste, Spicy Chili Oil, cayenne pepper, paprika, cinnamon, cumin, cloves, sugar, 1¾ cups of the coconut milk, and the fish sauce in a large, well-seasoned pan. Bring to a boil over medium-high heat. Cook for 5 minutes, until all the ingredients are combined, stirring occasionally.

Add the remaining 3½ cups of coconut milk one cup at a time, bringing the sauce back to a vigorous boil after each addition. Mix thoroughly.

Reduce the sauce for 25 to 30 minutes, until the oil starts to appear on the surface. Stir only to prevent sticking or burning. If necessary to prevent sticking, add 2 tablespoons of Chicken Stock; repeat as needed.

Add the peanut butter and 4 tablespoons of Chicken Stock. Stir well. Continue to reduce the sauce until 1 tablespoon of the oil surfaces; quickly remove from heat.

Serve ½ cup on a flat dish as a dipping sauce for 6 to 8 skewers of Beef Satay.

Makes approximately 3 cups.

LIME SAUCE
(Nam Manow)

Lime Sauce is very common in Thailand. It is garlicky and goes nicely with most seafoods and fried foods. Adjust the amount of Thai chili peppers according to your taste. This sauce is easy to make. It will keep in the refrigerator for 1 day, but is best when freshly made.

> ¼ cup fish sauce
> ¼ cup fresh lime juice
> 1 medium clove garlic, finely chopped
> 3 Thai chili peppers, thinly sliced into rings
> Pinch of sugar

Combine all ingredients in a small bowl, stir to dissolve sugar, and serve.

> Makes ½ cup.

SHRIMP PASTE SAUCE
(Nam Prik Gabee)

In Thailand, Shrimp Paste Sauce is used as a dipping sauce for fresh vegetables and pan-fried mackerel. It is very hot and intensely flavored. To control the hotness and texture of the various ingredients, use a mortar to prepare this recipe. Since crushing the chili peppers releases more of their heat, temper it by crushing them only slightly. Refrigerated in a sealed container, this sauce will keep indefinitely.

> ¼ cup dried shrimp
> 3 large cloves garlic (approximately 1 ounce)
> ½ cup shrimp paste
> 2 tablespoons sugar
> ¾ cup fresh lime juice
> 20 Thai chili peppers, stems removed
> Rind of 1 lime
> ¼ cup plus 2 tablespoons boiled water, cooled to room temperature

In a large mortar pound the dried shrimp to fine pieces. Add the garlic and pound to fine pieces. Add the shrimp paste, sugar, and lime juice, combining all the ingredients well. Add the chili peppers and crush. Add ¼ cup of the water and combine. Pour into a serving bowl and set aside.

Add 2 tablespoons of water to the mortar to clean the sides. Turn the lime rind inside out. Use the cut edge to scrape out the remaining sauce and add it to the serving bowl. This gives the sauce a slight lime fragrance. Discard the rind.

Slivered lime rind may be added to the sauce if it is to be consumed right away. Do not leave the slivers in the sauce overnight, or it will become very bitter.

Makes 1¾ cups.

Pork

 ## PORK WITH HOT PEPPERS
(Mu Pat Prik Sot)

The chili peppers in this recipe turn an otherwise ordinary dish into something wonderful. Adjust the number of peppers according to your taste, but don't eliminate them completely. This dish is very easy to make.

> 1¾ teaspoons cornstarch
> 1 tablespoon water
> 8 ounces lean pork, sliced into thin, bite-sized pieces
> 2 green jalapeño or serrano chili peppers
> 2 red jalapeño chili peppers
> 3 tablespoons oil
> 1 tablespoon minced garlic
> ¼ wedge medium yellow onion (approximately 2 ounces)
> 5 medium button mushrooms, sliced (approximately 2 ounces)
> 1½ tablespoons oyster sauce

Combine the cornstarch and water in a small bowl. Add 1 teaspoon of the cornstarch mixture to the sliced pork and mix until all of the liquid is absorbed. Set aside. (Save the rest of the cornstarch mixture for use in other recipes.)

Remove the stems from the chili peppers and cut lengthwise into quarters. Set aside.

Heat a well-seasoned pan over high heat and add the oil. When oil is hot, add the garlic and onion. Sauté until the garlic is light brown.

Add the pork, chili peppers, and mushrooms; stir quickly. Add the oyster sauce and stir-fry for 2 to 3 minutes, until the pork is just done. Serve immediately.

Serves 4.

GREEN CURRY PORK
(Gang Keow Waan Mu)

Like the Chili Pepper Salad, Green Curry Pork comes with a
warning. It is hot, very hot. It is so hot that in 1985 it won the "Some
Like It Hotter" contest sponsored by the Anchor Steam Brewing Company in San Francisco. It was rated the "hottest and tastiest" entry. Unlike
the Chili Pepper Salad, however, the Green Curry Pork looks ominous
because of the dark green oil that rises to the surface. At the restaurant,
it is the most frequently ordered pork dish. Beef, chicken, or whole fish
may be substituted. The finished dish can be stored in the refrigerator
for 1 to 2 days.

> 1½ pounds lean pork, sliced into thin, bite-sized pieces
> 2½ cups water
> Green Curry Paste (page 80)
> 1½ teaspoons sugar
> 3 tablespoons fish sauce
> 2½ cups thick coconut milk
> ½ cup fresh peas (optional)
> 30 Thai or Italian basil leaves
> 1 jalapeño chili pepper, sliced lengthwise into quarters

Parboil the pork in the water for 2 minutes, until it is just done. Drain
the pork, reserving the stock, and set aside.

In a large, well-seasoned wok or pan, combine the Green Curry Paste,
sugar, fish sauce, and 1 cup of the coconut milk. Bring to a boil and
reduce over medium-high heat for 15 to 20 minutes. Scrape the sides
and bottom of the pan as needed to prevent sticking or burning as
the mixture becomes dry and pasty.

Tiny pockets of oil from the coconut milk should start to surface at this
time. If the oil does not surface, add 3 to 4 tablespoons of the pork
stock and bring to a boil. Reduce for 3 to 4 minutes. Repeat if
necessary.

Cook for another 10 minutes at medium-high heat, scraping the sides
and bottom of the pan. Add the rest of the coconut milk and 1 cup
of the pork stock. Just before the curry begins to boil again, add the
pork and the peas, if used. Bring to a vigorous boil. Remove from
the stove and add the basil leaves. Stir, garnish with the chili pepper,
and serve immediately.

Serves 6.

If other meats are substituted for the pork, proceed in the same manner, parboiling the meat and using either 1 cup of the stock from the meat or fresh Chicken Stock (page 53).

When using fish, eliminate the parboiling. Continue with the recipe, substituting 1½ cups of fresh Chicken Stock for the cup of meat stock and bring to a boil. Add the fish and bring to a boil again. Do not stir. Continue cooking at high heat without stirring for 10 to 12 minutes, until the fish is done. Remove from the stove, garnish, and serve immediately.

GINGER PORK
(Pat King Mu)

This mild dish is very popular at the restaurant and goes well with any meal. The actual cooking time is very short, so be sure to prepare all the ingredients in advance.

> ¼ ounce small dried black fungus (cloud ears)
> 1¾ teaspoons cornstarch
> 1 tablespoon water
> 6½ ounces lean pork, sliced into thin, bite-sized pieces
> 1½ tablespoons oil
> ½ teaspoon garlic, smashed and minced
> 1 teaspoon bean sauce
> 2-inch section fresh ginger, peeled and sliced into fine julienne pieces (approximately 1½ ounces)
> ½ medium yellow onion, cut into quarters
> Pinch of ground white pepper
> 2 tablespoons oyster sauce
> ½ tablespoon Kwan's Sweet and Sour Sauce (page 87)
> ¼ teaspoon white vinegar
> 2 green onions, sliced into 2-inch lengths
> 3 tablespoons fresh Chicken Stock (page 53)

Soak the black fungus in a small bowl of water for 5 to 10 minutes until tender. Drain and set aside.

Combine the cornstarch and water in a small bowl. Add 1 teaspoon of the cornstarch mixture to the pork and mix until all of the liquid is absorbed. Set aside. (Save the rest of the cornstarch mixture for use in other recipes.)

Heat a well-seasoned pan or wok over high heat and add the oil. When oil is hot, add the garlic, bean sauce, and ginger in order. Sauté until the garlic is light brown.

Quickly add the pork, black fungus, yellow onion, white pepper, and oyster sauce. Flip the ingredients in the pan several times to stir. Add the sweet and sour sauce, vinegar, green onions, and Chicken Stock. Stir-fry for 2½ to 3 minutes until the pork is well done. Serve immediately.

     Serves 4.

PRINCESS FAVORITE PORK
(Breow Waan Mu)

Princess Favorite Pork is the Thai version of Chinese sweet and sour pork. It has a thick, rich sauce and is very easy to make.

    4 teaspoons cornstarch
    2 tablespoons water
    2½ tablespoons oil
    1 tablespoon minced garlic
    ¼ wedge medium yellow onion
    ½ small bell pepper, sliced into angular pieces
    6 pineapple chunks
    1 cup fresh Chicken Stock (page 53)
    5 ounces lean pork, sliced into thin, bite-sized pieces
    3 tablespoons fish sauce
    2 tablespoons Kwan's Sweet and Sour Sauce (page 87)
    2 tablespoons catsup
    ½ small tomato, cut into 3 sections
    1 green onion, cut into 2-inch lengths

Combine the cornstarch and water in a small bowl and set aside.

Heat a well-seasoned pan or wok over high heat and add the oil. When oil is hot, add the garlic and sauté until light brown.

Add the yellow onion, bell pepper, and pineapple chunks. Stir-fry for a few seconds. Add the Chicken Stock, pork, and cornstarch mixture in order. Stir. Add the fish sauce, sweet and sour sauce, catsup, tomato, and green onion. Stir-fry for 2 to 3 minutes, until the pork is well done. Serve immediately.

     Serves 4.

PORK AND GREEN BEANS IN RED CURRY PASTE
(Pat Prik King Mu)

Pork and Green Beans in Red Curry Paste has a thick, grainy hot sauce which must be stirred often to prevent it from burning. When the curry paste is reduced, the oil takes on a deep red color, giving it its attractive "hot" look.

> 3 tablespoons dried shrimp (approximately ½ ounce)
> ½ cup oil
> Red Curry Paste II (page 82)
> ¼ teaspoon salt
> 2 tablespoons plus 1 teaspoon sugar
> ⅓ teaspoon shrimp paste
> ¼ cup plus 3 tablespoons fish sauce
> ½ cup fresh Chicken Stock (page 53)
> 10 to 12 ounces Blue Lake green beans, cut into 2½-inch lengths
> 10 to 12 ounces lean pork, sliced into thin, bite-sized pieces

In a blender grind the dried shrimp into fine pieces. Reserve 1½ tablespoons, and set aside.

Heat a well-seasoned pan or wok over high heat and add the oil. When the oil is hot, add the curry paste, ground shrimp, salt, sugar, shrimp paste, and fish sauce; stir well. Reduce over high heat for 10 minutes, until the oil surfaces. Stir as needed to prevent burning.

Lower the heat to medium low and cook at a very low boil for another 20 minutes, stirring as needed. Cover the pan with the lid ajar, to keep the splattering down.

If the mixture gets too dry and starts to stick, add ¼ cup of the Chicken Stock. Repeat if necessary.

While the curry mixture cooks, parboil the green beans for 3 seconds; drain.

Add the pork and green beans to the curry. Cook over medium-high heat for 5 to 7 minutes, until the pork and green beans are done. Serve immediately.

Serves 6 to 8.

BRAISED SPARERIBS
(Graduk Mu Pat Pong Garee)

This particular recipe is not Thai; it is prepared mostly in the kitchens of Chinese living in Thailand. The spareribs are braised until the meat is tender and succulent and the spices become a harmonious blend. The rich, yellow-brown gravy is excellent over rice.

> 1½ to 1¾ pounds lean pork spareribs
> ½ tablespoon cornstarch
> ½ tablespoon water
> 4 tablespoons oil
> 2 tablespoons minced garlic
> 1 tablespoon ground white pepper
> 2 ounces fresh ginger, peeled and sliced into fine julienne pieces
> 2 teaspoons yellow curry powder
> 2 tablespoons fish sauce
> 2 tablespoons sugar
> 1 to 2 cups fresh Chicken Stock (page 53)

Have the butcher cut the spareribs into 2-inch lengths. Cut into individual ribs and set aside.

Combine the cornstarch and water and set aside.

Heat a large, well-seasoned pan or wok over high heat and add 1 tablespoon of the oil. Add the spareribs and brown. Remove and drain well, leaving all the drippings in the pan. Set the spareribs aside.

Add the rest of the oil to the pan and heat over medium-high heat. Add the garlic, white pepper, and ginger in order and sauté for 4 to 5 minutes, until you can smell the ingredients.

Add 1 teaspoon of the yellow curry powder and stir. Add the browned spareribs; cook for 1 minute. Add the remaining teaspoon of curry powder, fish sauce, and sugar. Mix, thoroughly coating the spareribs.

Add 1 cup of the Chicken Stock and turn the heat to medium. Cover and cook for 1 minute until the meat starts to shrink on the bones. Add the cornstarch mixture and stir. Cover and cook for 15 to 20 minutes, until the meat can be easily pulled from the bone and oil separates from the thick gravy. Check occasionally, adding more Chicken

Stock if necessary so that the dish does not dry out completely. There should be about ½ cup of gravy remaining. Serve immediately.

Serves 4 to 6.

 THAI BARBECUED SPARERIBS
(Graduk Mu Yang)

Thai Barbecued Spareribs are very easy to prepare and are excellent for outdoor gatherings. To keep the ribs moist, they are partially baked in the oven. They can be prepared in advance up to this point and kept in the refrigerator for up to 4 days. Grill them over hot coals just before serving.

¼ cup Golden Mountain Sauce
½ cup soy sauce
¾ cup red wine
6 tablespoons sugar
1 tablespoon ground black pepper
1 tablespoon finely minced garlic
2-inch piece fresh ginger, crushed
2 tablespoons sesame oil
2½ to 3 pounds lean pork spareribs

Combine the Golden Mountain Sauce, soy sauce, red wine, sugar, black pepper, garlic, ginger, and sesame oil in a flat pan large enough to hold the spareribs.

Place the spareribs in the pan and marinate overnight in the refrigerator. Turn the spareribs once, so that both sides are marinated.

Preheat the oven to 350°. Bake the spareribs for 25 minutes, removing them before they are done.

To complete the cooking, light a charcoal grill to an even, medium-high heat. Adjust the grill to 3 to 4 inches above the coals. Grill the ribs for 7 minutes on each side.

To serve, slice into individual ribs.

Serves 6 to 8.

SWEET PORK
(Mu Waan)

Sweet Pork has a very intense flavor and is usually served at breakfast to accompany Plain Rice Soup (page 62). It can, however, be eaten at any meal. The pork is cooked until the meat is well done and the sauce is reduced to a very thick and sticky consistency. Chicken may be substituted, but we prefer to make this dish with pork. It is very quick to prepare and makes a tasty, last-minute addition to any meal.

        4 tablespoons oil
        1½ tablespoons minced garlic
        14 ounces lean pork, sliced into thin, bite-sized pieces
        ½ tablespoon ground white pepper
        3 tablespoons Golden Mountain sauce
        2 tablespoons fish sauce
        3 tablespoons sugar

Heat a well-seasoned pan or wok over high heat and add the oil. When oil is hot, add the garlic, pork, and white pepper in order. Stir-fry for a few seconds. Add the Golden Mountain sauce and fish sauce; stir-fry for 30 seconds. Add the sugar; stir-fry for 3 to 4 minutes, until the sauce thickens and adheres to the pork, completely coating it. Serve immediately.

        Serves 4.

THAI EGG FOO YUNG
(Kai Jeow Mu Sap)

Thai Egg Foo Yung is similar to the deep-fried Chinese version. It is pan-fried and rises into a very light and fluffy omelet. Drain the omelet for a few seconds on paper towels and transfer it immediately to a serving plate; it tends to get soggy if left on the paper towels. This dish is sometimes served with Lime Sauce (page 93).

4 large eggs

2 ounces lean ground pork *or* one 10-ounce jar of small oysters,
    well drained

1 small green onion, thinly sliced (approximately 2 teaspoons)

2 teaspoons fish sauce

1 teaspoon Golden Mountain sauce

¼ teaspoon water

⅛ teaspoon ground white pepper

½ cup plus 2 tablespoons oil

Combine the eggs, pork or oysters, green onion, fish sauce, Golden
    Mountain sauce, water, and white pepper in a bowl. Beat together
    until the pork is broken into smaller pieces.

Heat a well-seasoned 8-inch omelet pan over high heat and add the oil.
    When oil is hot, carefully pour in the egg mixture. It will puff up
    immediately. Reduce the heat to medium. Scramble the center,
    allowing it to rise. When browned, use two spatulas to turn the
    omelet. Brown the other side.

Use a slotted spatula to remove the omelet from the oil and drain on
    several paper towels. Transfer to a serving plate and serve immediately.

Serves 4.

Beef and Lamb

BEEF WITH HOT PEPPERS
(Nuar Pat Prik Sod)

This is the hot version of Chinese beef with oyster sauce. The jalapeño chili peppers completely transform the flavor, and are necessary to the end result. You can reduce the number of chili peppers according to your taste, but don't eliminate them completely. The red ones are slightly sweeter than green ones, and also add more color.

> 7½ ounces flank steak
> 1¾ teaspoons cornstarch
> 1 tablespoon water
> 2 green jalapeño or serrano chili peppers
> 2 red jalapeño chili peppers
> 1½ tablespoons oil
> 1 tablespoon minced garlic
> ¼ wedge medium yellow onion (approximately 1½ to 2 ounces)
> 5 medium button mushrooms, sliced (approximately 1½ to 2 ounces)
> 1½ tablespoons oyster sauce

Slice the flank steak across the grain. Holding the knife at an angle, cut into bite-sized pieces approximately 1¾ by 1½ by ¹⁄₁₆ inch thick. Place in a small bowl and set aside.

Combine the cornstarch and water in a small bowl. Add 1 teaspoon to the sliced steak. (Save the rest of the cornstarch mixture for use in other recipes.) Mix until all the liquid is absorbed by the beef. Set aside.

Remove the stems from the chili peppers and cut lengthwise into quarters. Set aside.

Heat a well-seasoned pan or wok over high heat and add the oil. When oil is hot, add the garlic and onion. Sauté until the garlic is light brown.

Add the flank steak, chili peppers, and mushrooms. Stir quickly, add the oyster sauce, and stir-fry for 2 minutes until the beef is just done. Serve immediately.

Serves 4.

PANANG BEEF
(Panang Nuar)

At the restaurant, Panang Beef is made by adding spices to the Basic Curry Paste. A rich, thick, red curry, this popular beef dish is hot, but Thais like to eat it hotter. If that's your preference too, just add more chili peppers to the recipe.

> 4 tablespoons Basic Curry Paste (page 79)
> 2½ teaspoons ground cayenne pepper
> 2 tablespoons paprika
> 1 teaspoon ground coriander
> ¼ teaspoon ground white pepper
> ¼ teaspoon ground cumin
> 4 tablespoons sugar
> 3 tablespoons fish sauce
> 3½ cups thick coconut milk
> 2 tablespoons creamy peanut butter
> 1 to 2 tablespoons fresh Chicken Stock (page 53)
> 13 to 14 ounces flank steak
> 1 fresh jalapeño or serrano chili pepper, stem removed and
>   sliced lengthwise into quarters
> 25 Thai or Italian basil leaves

In a large, well-seasoned pan or wok combine the curry paste, cayenne pepper, paprika, coriander, white pepper, cumin, sugar, fish sauce, and 1¾ cups of the coconut milk. Reduce the curry over medium-high heat for 30 to 50 minutes until it becomes dry and pasty and tiny pockets of red oil appear on the surface. Scrape the sides and bottom of the pan as necessary to prevent sticking or burning.

Add the remaining 1¾ cups of coconut milk ½ cup at a time. Stir the coconut milk completely into the curry after each addition. Cook for another 10 minutes, until the red oil reappears.

Add the peanut butter and cook for another 5 minutes. If the mixture
gets too dry and starts to stick, add 1 tablespoon of the Chicken
Stock. Repeat if necessary.

Slice the flank steak across the grain. Holding the knife at an angle, cut
into bite-sized pieces approximately 1¾ by 1½ by ¹⁄₁₆ inch thick.

Add the flank steak and chili pepper to the curry. Cook at high heat for
1 to 2 minutes, until the beef is medium done. Remove from heat
and add the Thai basil. Stir and serve immediately.

Serves 6 to 8.

 ## MUSUMAN CURRY
(Musuman Nuar)

Musuman Curry is a rich, hearty beef stew from Southern Thailand. It is a Muslim curry and uses many spices not common to other
Thai curries. Its fragrance and flavor deteriorate rapidly, so it should not
be kept past the second day. If not served immediately, add 1 to 2 tablespoons of Spicy Chili Oil to heighten the flavor. In this recipe Kwan boils
the beef first in coconut milk to stop it from shrinking too much.

> 3 ounces preserved tamarind
> ¾ cup hot water
> 3 tablespoons raw peanuts
> 5 tablespoons oil
> Musuman Curry Paste (page 86)
> 2½ tablespoons Spicy Chili Oil (page 89)
> 5 tablespoons sugar
> 10 tablespoons fish sauce
> ¼ teaspoon ground white pepper
> 5¼ cups thick coconut milk
> 4 to 4½ pounds lean chuck roast, cut into 1½- to 2-inch cubes
> 5 bay leaves
> 3 to 4 whole cardamom pods, wrapped in cheesecloth
> 1¾ cups fresh Chicken Stock (page 53)
> 1 large potato
> 6 to 12 pearl onions

In a small bowl soak the tamarind in the hot water for 30 minutes, until
soft. Work the tamarind with your hands for 10 minutes to release

the pulp. Press the pulp through a strainer, squeezing out all the liquid and pulp, and discard the twigs and seeds. Reserve 5¼ table-spoons and set aside.

Dry-roast the peanuts in a skillet for 10 minutes over medium-low heat until evenly browned, flipping frequently. Set aside.

Heat a well-seasoned pan over medium heat and add the oil. When the oil is hot, add the Musuman Curry Paste. Sauté for 15 minutes, being careful not to let it burn.

Add the Spicy Chili Oil, sugar, fish sauce, white pepper, and 1¾ cups of the coconut milk. Reduce over medium heat for 30 minutes, until tiny pockets of oil from the coconut milk start to surface. Scrape the sides and bottom of the pan as needed to prevent burning. Turn off the heat and set aside.

Place the chuck roast, bay leaves, and remaining 3½ cups of coconut milk in a medium stockpot. Cover and bring to a vigorous boil over medium-high heat. Boil for 3 minutes.

Add the peanuts, cardamom pods, Chicken Stock, and contents of the pan to the stockpot. Cover and boil for another 25 minutes. Turn the heat to low and simmer for 1 to 1½ hours, until the meat is tender. Stir occasionally to keep it from sticking or burning. There should be a thin layer of oil on the surface.

While the meat is cooking, boil the potato. Peel and cut it into 1½-inch cubes. When the meat is tender, add the potato and onions and simmer for another 3 minutes. Remove the cardamom pods and serve.

Serves 6 to 8.

 ## BEEF WITH OYSTER SAUCE
(Pat Nuar Nam Mun Hoi)

Beef with Oyster Sauce is a mild dish that incorporates many different textures. It is similar to the Chinese version and is very quick and easy to make.

5 ounces flank steak
1¼ teaspoons cornstarch
1 tablespoon water

2½ tablespoons oil
1 tablespoon minced garlic
¼ teaspoon ground white pepper
3 tablespoons oyster sauce
3 baby corn, sliced in half lengthwise
¼ medium yellow onion
3 water chestnuts, sliced
3 medium button mushrooms, sliced ¼ inch thick
¼ cup fresh Chicken Stock (page 53)
⅛ teaspoon sugar
1 green onion, cut into 2-inch lengths
⅛ teaspoon sesame oil

Slice the flank steak across the grain. Holding the knife at an angle, cut into bite-sized pieces approximately 1¾ by 1½ by ¹⁄₁₆ inch thick. Set aside.

In a small bowl combine the cornstarch and water. Set aside.

Heat a well-seasoned pan or wok over high heat and add the oil. When oil is hot, add the garlic and white pepper. Sauté until the garlic is light brown.

Add the beef, oyster sauce, and cornstarch mixture; stir-fry until the beef absorbs most of the liquid.

Add the baby corn, yellow onion, water chestnuts, and mushrooms. Stir-fry for about 1½ minutes, until the beef is almost done. Add the Chicken Stock, sugar, and green onion. Stir-fry for another ½ minute, until the beef is done. Remove from heat, add the sesame oil, and serve immediately.

Serves 4.

 IMPERIAL BEEF
(Nuar Pat Kana)

Imperial Beef is stir-fried with broccoli in a mild sweet and sour sauce. It is easy to make.

8 ounces broccoli

3 ounces flank steak

3½ teaspoons cornstarch

2 tablespoons water

2 tablespoons oil

1 tablespoon minced garlic

1½ teaspoons bean sauce

⅛ teaspoon ground white pepper

2 tablespoons oyster sauce

6 tablespoons fresh Chicken Stock (page 53)

2 tablespoons Kwan's Sweet and Sour Sauce (page 87)

½ teaspoon white vinegar

⅛ teaspoon sesame oil

To prepare the broccoli, cut the flowers 2½ inches from the top and separate into smaller sections. Peel the stem and cut into rectangular pieces about 3 by 1¼ by ³⁄₁₆ inch. Blanch the broccoli for about 10 seconds. Drain and set aside.

Slice the flank steak across the grain. Holding the knife at an angle, cut into bite-sized pieces approximately 1¾ by 1½ by ¹⁄₁₆ inch thick. Set aside.

In a small bowl combine the cornstarch and water. Reserve 1½ tablespoons and set aside. (Save the rest of the cornstarch mixture for use in other recipes.)

Heat a well-seasoned pan or wok over high heat and add the oil. When oil is hot, add the garlic and bean sauce. Sauté until the garlic is light brown.

Add the beef, white pepper, oyster sauce, and cornstarch mixture in order. Stir-fry for 15 seconds, until the beef has absorbed the liquids.

Add the broccoli and stir-fry for 15 seconds. Add the Chicken Stock, sweet and sour sauce, and vinegar. Stir-fry for another 20 seconds. Remove from heat, add the sesame oil, and serve immediately.

Serves 4.

SALTY BEEF
(Nuar Kem)

In Thailand, thin slices of beef are dried outdoors for one day on flat bamboo baskets. The meat is marinated overnight, cooked, and sold as salty beef. This recipe is slightly sweeter and the beef thicker than the salty beef available in Thailand. It is eaten by shredding off pieces of the beef, very much like beef jerky. However, it is moist and tender, not dry and chewy.

> 1½ pounds flank steak
> ¼ cup minced garlic
> 5 tablespoons Golden Mountain sauce
> 5 tablespoons oyster sauce
> 1 tablespoon ground white pepper
> 1 tablespoon ground coriander
> 1 teaspoon sugar
> 2 tablespoons oil

Cut the flank steak along the grain into strips 2 inches wide. Cut each strip into pieces 5 inches long and set aside.

In a bowl large enough to hold the beef combine the garlic, Golden Mountain sauce, oyster sauce, white pepper, coriander, and sugar.

Add the flank steak and mix until thoroughly coated. Marinate for at least 2 hours, or up to 3 days.

Heat a well-seasoned pan over medium to medium-low heat and add the oil. When oil is hot, add the flank steak and fry for 16 to 17 minutes until well-done, browning all sides. Be careful not to let it burn.

Serve hot or at room temperature in whole pieces.

Serves 4 to 6.

RACK OF LAMB
(Gae Yang)

At Siam Cuisine, rack of lamb is used for this recipe because of its high quality and low fat content. However, rib or loin chops may be substituted. Rack of Lamb is very easy to prepare. The lamb is marinated in lemon juice, honey, and yellow curry powder, which reduces the gamey flavor. It is then grilled over hot coals.

> 1 rack of lamb (approximately 3 to 4 pounds)
> 3 to 5 large lemons
> ½ cup honey
> 2 to 3 medium onions, finely chopped
> 3 tablespoons yellow curry powder
> 3 tablespoons ground coriander
> 1 tablespoon salt
> Water

Slice the rack of lamb into individual chops, or have your butcher do it for you. Set aside.

Cut the lemons in half and squeeze the juice into a bowl large enough to hold the lamb. Discard the seeds; set the rinds aside. Add the honey, onions, yellow curry powder, coriander, and salt. Stir until the honey is completely dissolved.

Add the rack of lamb, lemon rinds, and enough water to cover completely. Stir. Marinate overnight or longer in the refrigerator.

Light a charcoal grill to an even, medium-high heat. Adjust the grill to 3 to 4 inches above the coals. Grill the lamb for 3 to 4 minutes on each side, or until medium done.

Serve immediately with Sriracha Chili Sauce.

Serves 6.

Thai fruits: bananas, coconuts, and pineapple

Spices and vegetables

Left: **Calamari Salad** *(Yum Bla Murk)* (recipe on page 66)
Right: **Hot and Sour Prawn Soup** *(Thom Yum Gung)* (recipe on page 54)

Shrimp Paste Sauce *(Nam Prik Gabee)* and vegetables (recipe on page 93)

Left: **Pork Wrapped in Tapioca Pearl** *(Saku Sai Mu)* (recipe on page 49)
Right: **Thai Crisp-fried Rice Threads** *(Mee Krob)* (recipe on page 46)

Beef Satay *(Nuar Satay)* (recipe on page 41)

Left: **Green Curry Fish with Krachai** *(Gang Keow Waan Bla Krachai)* (recipe on page 145). Right: **Ground Prawn Curry with Somen Noodles** *(Kanom Jean Nam Prik)* (recipe on page 165)

Barbequed Chicken *(Gai Yang)* (recipe on page 122) and **Green Papaya Salad** *(Som Tham Mara Gor)* (recipe on page 74)

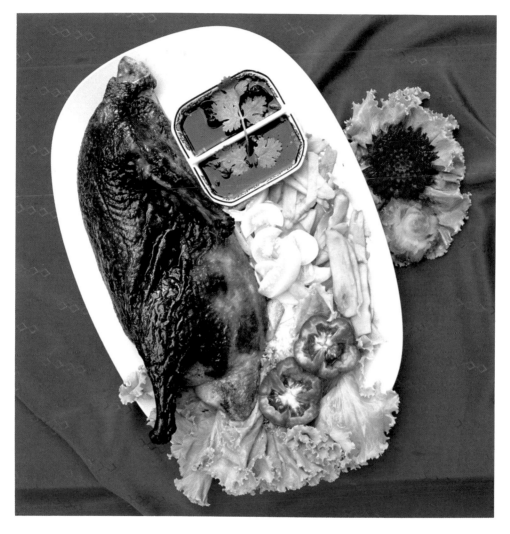

Siam Roast Duck *(Baet Yang)* (recipe on page 120)

Panang Beef *(Panang Nuar)* (recipe on page 106)

Chicken with Bamboo Shoots *(Gai Pat Pet Nar Mai)* (recipe on page 114)

Left: **Pork and Green Beans in Red Curry Paste** *(Pat Prik Chua Mu)* (recipe on page 99). Right: **Fried Fish with Spicy Sauce** *(Bla Tot Lat Prik)* (recipe on page 134)

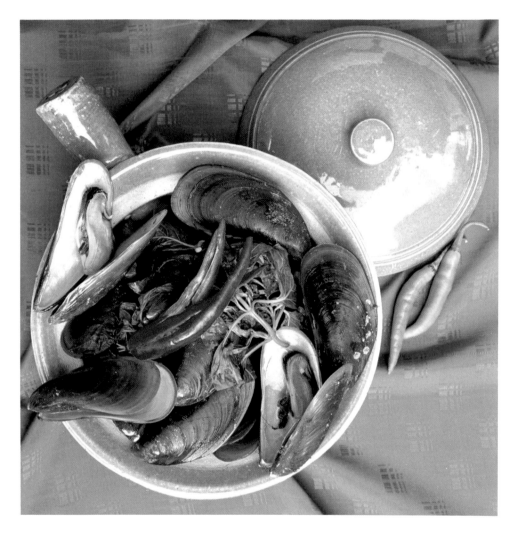

Mussel Clay Pot *(Hoy Malang Phu Mar Din)* (recipe on page 152)

Thai Noodles *(Phat Thai)* (recipe on page 158)

Coconut Pudding in Banana Leaf Cup *(Grob Kem)* (recipe on page 171)

Steamed Tapioca Cake *(Kanom Chan)* (recipe on page 175)

Poultry

 CHICKEN WITH SWEET BASIL
(Gai Pat Bai Grapraow)

Chicken with Sweet Basil is hot but it is one of the more popular chicken dishes at Siam Cuisine. In Thailand, this dish is made with holy basil, which has a very delicate clove flavor. Because holy basil was not available when the restaurant first opened, orange bergamot mint, which has more of an anise flavor, was substituted. It is still used at the restaurant, having become a standard for their customers' palates.

> 2 dried cayenne peppers
> 1 tablespoon oil
> 1 teaspoon minced garlic
> 10 ounces boned, skinned chicken breast, sliced into thin, bite-sized pieces
> Pinch of ground white pepper
> 3 jalapeño or serrano chili peppers, stems removed, cut lengthwise into quarters
> 2 tablespoons oyster sauce
> ⅛ teaspoon sugar
> 1 cup fresh holy basil leaves, loosely packed *or* 25 to 30 orange mint or orange bergamot mint leaves

Soak the dried cayenne peppers in hot water for about 15 minutes, until soft. Drain and chop into small pieces. Reserve ½ teaspoon and set aside.

Heat a well-seasoned pan or wok over high heat and add the oil. When oil is hot, add the garlic and cayenne peppers. Sauté until the garlic is light brown.

Quickly add the chicken, white pepper, and chili peppers. Stir-fry for 10 seconds. Add the oyster sauce and sugar. Stir-fry for 2 to 3 minutes, until the chicken is medium done. Add the basil leaves and stir-fry for another 10 seconds. Serve immediately.

Serves 4.

CHICKEN WITH BAMBOO SHOOTS
(Gai Pat Pet Nar Mai)

Chicken with Bamboo Shoots is another hot stir-fry dish which is very quick and easy to prepare. It incorporates a variety of ingredients including Thai basil, which is added at the end.

> 2 to 3 dried cayenne peppers
> 1½ tablespoons oil
> ½ teaspoon finely minced garlic
> 10 ounces boned, skinned chicken breast, sliced into thin, bite-sized pieces
> 2 jalapeño or serrano chili peppers, stems removed, cut lengthwise into quarters
> ¼ red bell pepper, cut into 4 or 5 triangular pieces
> 3 to 4 ounces bamboo shoots, cut into 10 wedges about ½ inch wide by 3 inches long
> 1⁄16 teaspoon ground white pepper
> 1½ tablespoons oyster sauce
> ¼ teaspoon sugar
> 1 green onion, cut into 2-inch lengths
> 20 Thai or Italian basil leaves

Soak the cayenne peppers in hot water for about 15 minutes, until soft. Drain and chop into small pieces. Reserve ½ teaspoon and set aside.

Heat a well-seasoned pan or wok over high heat and add the oil. When oil is hot, add the garlic and cayenne peppers; sauté until the garlic is light brown.

Quickly add the chicken, chili peppers, bell pepper, bamboo shoots, and white pepper; stir-fry a few seconds. Add the oyster sauce and sugar. Stir-fry for 2 to 3 minutes, until the chicken is medium done. Add the green onion and Thai basil leaves. Stir-fry until the leaves are wilted. Serve immediately.

Serves 4.

RED CURRY CHICKEN
(Gang Pet Gai)

Red Curry Chicken is a hot dish that in Thailand is made with almost any type of meat, whole fish, or foul. When the curry paste is reduced, it should become a thick, dark, grainy consistency. The curry will keep for 2 to 3 days in the refrigerator. To reheat, bring to a vigorous boil and turn off the heat immediately.

> 1½ pounds boned, skinned chicken breast, sliced into thin, bite-sized pieces
> 2 to 2½ cups fresh Chicken Stock (page 53)
> Red Curry Paste I (page 81)
> 2 teaspoons sugar
> 3 tablespoons fish sauce
> 2½ cups thick coconut milk
> 6 to 10 ounces bamboo shoots, cut lengthwise into 20 to 30 wedges about ½ by 3 inches (optional)
> 4 jalapeño or serrano chili peppers, stems removed, cut lengthwise into quarters
> 1 cup Thai or Italian basil leaves, loosely packed (approximately 60 leaves)

Parboil the chicken in the Chicken Stock for 2 minutes, until it is just done. Remove the chicken, reserving the stock. Set aside.

Add the curry paste, sugar, fish sauce, and 1 cup of the coconut milk to a large well-seasoned pan or wok. Bring to a boil and reduce over medium-high heat for 15 to 20 minutes, scraping the sides and bottom of the pan as needed to prevent sticking or burning as the mixture becomes dry and pasty.

Tiny pockets of oil from the coconut milk should start to surface at this time. If the oil does not surface, add 3 to 4 tablespoons of the reserved chicken stock and bring to a boil. Reduce for 3 to 4 minutes. Repeat if necessary.

Cook for another 10 minutes at medium-high heat, scraping the sides and bottom of the pan. Add the remaining 1½ cups coconut milk and 1 cup of the reserved chicken stock. Just before the curry starts to boil again, add the chicken and bamboo shoots. Bring to a vigorous boil. Do not stir. Remove from stove and add the chili peppers and Thai basil leaves. Stir and serve immediately.

Serves 6 to 8.

If other meats are substituted, proceed in the same manner, parboiling
    the meat.
When using fish, eliminate the parboiling. Continue the recipe, adding
    the fish, and bring to a boil again. Do not stir. Continue cooking at
    high heat without stirring for 10 to 12 minutes until the fish is done.
    Remove from stove, add the chili peppers and basil, and serve
    immediately.

 YELLOW CURRY CHICKEN
(Gang Garee Gai)

Yellow Curry Chicken is the most popular chicken dish served
at Siam Cuisine. It is medium hot. Occasionally in the preparation of this
recipe, the oil from the coconut milk will not surface even after the
chicken stock is added. If this occurs, add another ½ cup of coconut milk
to the paste and reduce for 10 minutes. Yellow Curry Chicken will keep
in the refrigerator for 1 to 2 days. To reheat, bring to a vigorous boil. If
it appears too thick, add some chicken stock.

> 1½ pounds boned, skinned chicken breast, sliced into thin,
>   bite-sized pieces
> 2½ cups fresh Chicken Stock (page 53)
> 2 large potatoes
> Yellow Curry Paste (page 85)
> 3 tablespoons fish sauce
> 2 teaspoons sugar
> 2½ cups thick coconut milk

Parboil the chicken in the Chicken Stock for 2 minutes, until it is just
    done. Remove the chicken, reserving the stock. Set aside.
Boil the potatoes until tender. Peel and cut into 1½-inch cubes. Set aside.
Place the Yellow Curry Paste, fish sauce, sugar, and 1 cup of the coconut
    milk in a large well-seasoned pan or wok. Bring to a boil and reduce
    over medium-high heat for 15 to 20 minutes, until the mixture starts
    to get dry and pasty. Scrape the sides and bottom of the pan as
    needed to prevent sticking or burning.
Tiny pockets of oil from the coconut milk should start to surface at this
    time. If the oil does not surface, add 3 to 4 tablespoons of the
    reserved chicken stock and bring to a boil. Reduce for 3 to 4 minutes.
    Repeat if necessary.

Cook for another 10 to 15 minutes at medium-high heat, stirring frequently. Add the remaining 1½ cups of coconut milk and 1 cup of the reserved chicken stock. Just before the curry starts to boil again, add the chicken and potatoes. Bring to a vigorous boil. Do not stir. Remove from stove and serve with Cucumber Salad (page 76).

Serves 6.

GINGER CHICKEN
(Gai Pat King)

Ginger Chicken is very popular at Siam Cuisine. It has a mild blend of flavors and is easy to prepare. To tone down the sharpness of the ginger, cut it into fine julienne pieces.

¼ ounce small dried black fungus (cloud ears)
1½ tablespoons oil
½ teaspoon garlic, smashed and minced
1 teaspoon bean sauce
2-inch section fresh ginger, peeled and sliced into fine julienne
    pieces (approximately 1½ ounces)
6½ ounces boned, skinned chicken breast, sliced into thin, bite-
    sized pieces
½ medium yellow onion, cut into quarters
Pinch of ground white pepper
2 tablespoons oyster sauce
½ tablespoon Kwan's Sweet and Sour Sauce (page 87)
¼ teaspoon white vinegar
2 green onions, sliced into 2-inch lengths
3 tablespoons fresh Chicken Stock (page 53)

Soak the black fungus in a small bowl of water for 5 to 10 minutes until
    tender. Drain and set aside.
Heat a well-seasoned pan or wok over high heat and add the oil. When
    oil is hot, add the garlic, bean sauce, and ginger in order. Sauté until
    the garlic is light brown.
Quickly add the chicken, black fungus, yellow onion, white pepper, and
    oyster sauce. Stir-fry for a few seconds. Add the sweet and sour
    sauce, vinegar, green onions, and Chicken Stock. Stir-fry for 2½ to
    3 minutes, until the chicken is done. Serve immediately.

Serves 4.

CHAU PRE YA CHICKEN
(Gai Pat Haet Sot Yot Kaopote)

Chau Pre Ya Chicken is stir-fried in a mild sweet and sour sauce and is very easy to prepare.

3½ teaspoons cornstarch
2 tablespoons water
1½ tablespoons oil
1 tablespoon minced garlic
1 tablespoon bean sauce
5 ounces boned, skinned chicken breast, sliced into thin, bite-sized pieces
4 water chestnuts, sliced
5 baby corn, cut in half lengthwise
5 medium button mushrooms, sliced
2 ounces sliced bamboo shoots
¼ medium yellow onion (approximately 2 ounces)
½ cup fresh Chicken Stock (page 53)
3 tablespoons oyster sauce
1½ tablespoons Kwan's Sweet and Sour Sauce (page 87)
½ teaspoon white vinegar
2 green onions, cut into 2-inch lengths
½ teaspoon sweet soy sauce
½ teaspoon sesame oil

Combine the cornstarch and water in a small bowl. Reserve 1½ tablespoons. (Save the rest of the cornstarch mixture for use in other recipes.)

Heat a well-seasoned pan or wok over high heat and add the oil. When oil is hot, add the garlic and bean sauce. Sauté until the garlic is light brown.

Quickly add the chicken, water chestnuts, baby corn, mushrooms, bamboo shoots, yellow onion, and Chicken Stock in order. Stir-fry for several seconds. Add the oyster sauce, sweet and sour sauce, white vinegar, and cornstarch mixture. Stir-fry for 1½ minutes. Add the green onions and sweet soy sauce. Stir-fry for another minute, until the chicken is done. Turn off the heat and add the sesame oil. Serve immediately.

Serves 4.

ANGEL WINGS
(Beek Gai Yat Sai)

These stuffed chicken wings can be served as an appetizer or as one course in a meal. This recipe uses chicken wings with the skin from the body still intact. Follow the directions for boning chicken (page 19), and save the wings with skin until you have accumulated enough for this recipe. The chicken wings can be stuffed and boiled in advance and kept in the refrigerator for up to 3 days before they are deep-fried.

> 12 ounces lean ground pork
> 2 tablespoons finely minced garlic
> 1½ teaspoons ground black pepper
> 3½ tablespoons fish sauce
> ½ tablespoon Golden Mountain sauce
> 6 tablespoons mung bean thread, soaked in water and cut into
>   1-inch lengths
> 6 chicken wings with body skin intact
> Oil for deep-frying

To make the filling, combine the pork, garlic, black pepper, fish sauce, Golden Mountain sauce, and mung bean thread in a bowl. Allow the mixture to stand for 1 hour to blend the flavors.

To bone the chicken wings, pull the skin and meat away from the end of the bone and cut off the cartilage at the widest point. Make several cuts into the end of the bone to sever the tendons. Pull the skin and meat down the bone, turning it inside out. Snap the bone from its socket and discard. Pull the skin down to expose the cartilage. Cut the cartilage from the end of the two remaining bones, being careful not to pierce the skin. Cut the tendon holding the two bone ends together. If necessary, make several cuts into the ends of the bones to sever the tendons. Work the meat down the length of the two bones. Snap them from their sockets and discard. Turn the wings right side out.

To stuff the chicken wings, divide the pork mixture into 6 equal portions. Stuff each wing. Lay each one on its side and flatten by spreading the meat evenly. With the wing still on its side, spread out the excess skin. Cut a flap, 3 by 3 inches, at the opening. Tuck this flap into the opening to keep the stuffing in place. Trim any excess skin. Set aside.

To cook the chicken wings, bring a large pot of water to a boil. Add the stuffed wings and start a timer at 18 minutes. Bring the water to a boil again, then turn the heat to low. Simmer at a low boil to prevent the skins from breaking. They should start to float. After 18 minutes, remove and drain.

In a deep-fryer, heat the oil to 400°. Deep-fry the chicken wings for 5 to 10 minutes, until crisp. Drain on paper towels.

Slice the wings into 3 or 4 pieces. Arrange on a platter and serve with Peanut and Cucumber Sauce (page 88).

Serves 4 to 6.

SIAM ROAST DUCK
(Baet Yang)

The meat of Siam Roast Duck is very tender and succulent. It absorbs the flavor of the stuffing liquid, which is also used as the base for the dipping sauce. The duck is inflated to separate the skin from the meat. This allows the fat to run off during roasting, leaving the skin slightly crisp. If you have trouble inflating the duck, check for tiny holes in the skin and repair them with needle and string.

> 4- to 5-pound duck including head and feet, dressed
> String
> 2-inch square piece dried tangerine peel
> 2 medium cloves garlic, minced
> 2 green onions, minced
> 2 or 3 slices fresh ginger, minced
> 2 whole fresh coriander plants, including roots, crushed slightly
> ¼ cup bean sauce
> ¼ cup *hoisin* sauce
> ¼ cup water
> 3 tablespoons soy sauce
> 2 tablespoons cooking sherry
> 2 teaspoons sugar
> Needle
> Drinking straw
> ¼ cup honey
> Iceberg or romaine lettuce

Discard any large pieces of fat in the cavity of the duck. Tie a piece of string securely around the neck of the duck below any incisions, but not so tightly that it cuts the skin. Set duck aside.

To prepare the stuffing liquid, soak the tangerine peel in a bowl of water until soft. Drain and mince. Combine the tangerine peel, garlic, green onions, ginger, coriander, bean sauce, *hoisin* sauce, water, soy sauce, sherry, and sugar in a small bowl.

Place the duck, head first, in a large bowl. Pour the stuffing liquid into the cavity. Sew up the opening with the needle and string so that it is airtight and none of the liquid or air escapes. Check the duck's skin for holes, and sew them up.

To inflate the duck, make a ½-inch incision on the neck below the string. Insert the drinking straw. (A bicycle pump may also be used.) Blow air into the cavity until the skin completely separates from the meat. Tie the neck again just below the incision so the air won't escape. Pat the duck dry.

In a large stockpot boil enough water to almost cover the duck. Reduce the heat to a simmer and add the honey.

Immerse the duck in the water for about 3 minutes, turning it with tongs to thoroughly coat it with honey. Remove the duck and hang it by the tail for 1 hour over a baking pan to catch any drippings. Repeat. This eliminates the need to baste the duck.

Preheat the oven to 400°. Place the duck on a rack over a roasting pan with the breast side up. Roast for 25 minutes. Pour off the fat that has accumulated in the pan. Turn the heat down to 350° and roast for another 25 minutes. Remove any accumulated fat. (If the wings or feet start to burn, cover them with aluminum foil.) Turn the heat up to 400°, turn the duck, and roast for another 20 minutes. When the duck is dark brown and slightly crisp, remove it from the oven. Allow it to cool for 10 to 15 minutes.

Drain the stuffing liquid into a bowl and set aside. Disjoint the duck and cut it in half lengthwise. Cut each half into 1½-inch pieces. Arrange the pieces on a bed of lettuce. Serve with Dipping Sauce (below).

Serves 6 to 8.

Siam Roast Duck Dipping Sauce
　　½ cup stuffing liquid (above)
　　3 tablespoons white vinegar
　　3 tablespoons soy sauce
　　¼ cup *hoisin* sauce

1 tablespoon fresh ginger, peeled and sliced into fine julienne
   pieces
1 to 2 jalapeño or serrano chili peppers, sliced into rings
Fresh coriander leaves

Combine the stuffing liquid, vinegar, soy sauce, *hoisin* sauce, and ginger in a bowl. Garnish with the chili peppers and coriander leaves.

BARBECUED CHICKEN
(Gai Yang)

The perfect "Barbecued Chicken" comes out of the oven with very crispy skin while the meat remains succulent and tender. The chicken is marinated in a blend of spices, grilled, and then finished in a hot oven. The marinating and grilling can be completed in advance; the baking saved until just before serving. This recipe also works well with cornish game hens. Adjust the grilling time to about 4 minutes per side.

Marinade

3 tablespoons thinly sliced galanga, fresh or frozen, firmly
   packed *or* ½ ounce dried
½ cup sliced garlic
3-inch section fresh lemon grass, thinly sliced
1¾ cup thick coconut milk
3 tablespoons Golden Mountain Sauce
3 tablespoons oyster sauce
½ teaspoon ground white pepper
1 tablespoon yellow curry powder
1 tablespoon sugar
1 tablespoon sesame oil

1 whole chicken (approximately 3½ pounds), cut in half

To prepare the marinade:
If dried galanga is used, soak it for 1 to 2 hours in hot water. Drain and
   slice thinly.
Place the galanga, garlic, and lemon grass in a mortar or blender. Pound
   or grind to a fine paste. If using a blender, add ½ cup of the liquid
   from the coconut milk which has separated from the cream to aid
   in the grinding process.

In a bowl large enough to hold the chicken, combine the paste, Golden
   Mountain Sauce, oyster sauce, white pepper, yellow curry powder,
   sugar, sesame oil, and coconut milk.

To complete the recipe:
Pat the chicken halves dry with a paper towel and place in the bowl,
   completely covering the chicken with the marinade. Allow to stand
   overnight in the refrigerator.
Light a charcoal grill to an even, high heat. Adjust the grill to 3 to 4 inches
   above the coals. Grill the chicken for about 7 minutes on each side,
   until grill marks show on the meat. Do not cook all the way.
Preheat the oven to 550° for about 20 minutes. Bake the grilled chicken
   for 17 minutes, until the skin is crisp.
Cut the chicken halves into several pieces and serve immediately with
   Thai Barbecued Chicken Sauce (page 89).

   Serves 6 to 8.

 ## GRILLED GARLIC QUAIL
(Nok Gata)

This recipe was a great favorite during Garlic Week in Berkeley,
California. It is prepared exactly like Barbecued Chicken (above); however, just before baking, each quail is coated with garlic oil.

   8 fresh quail
   Marinade for Barbecued Chicken (page 122)
   4 tablespoons oil
   8 teaspoons chopped garlic
   2 teaspoons white pepper
   ⅜ teaspoon salt

Pat the quail dry with paper towels and place in a large bowl. Add the
   Marinade, completely covering the birds. Allow to stand overnight
   in the refrigerator.
Light a charcoal grill to an even, high heat. Adjust the grill to 3 to 4 inches
   above the coals. Grill the quail for 2 to 3 minutes per side, until grill
   marks show. Do not cook all the way. Place quail in a baking pan
   and set aside.
Preheat the oven to 550° for about 20 minutes.

Place the oil, garlic, white pepper, and salt in a well-seasoned pan. Sauté over medium heat until the garlic is light brown, being careful not to let it burn. Remove from the stove and allow to cool. Dip each quail in the oil to coat thoroughly.

Bake the quail for 7 minutes. Serve with Thai Barbecued Chicken Sauce (page 89).

Serves 4.

 ## RED WINE CHICKEN WINGS
(Beek Gai Laow Dang)

In Thailand these chicken wings are cooked with Thai whiskey; this recipe calls for red wine. The sauce can be prepared in advance and stored in the refrigerator for 2 to 3 days, but bring it to room temperature before using. The chicken wings can also be marinated and steamed in advance, leaving the deep-frying until just before serving.

12 chicken wings
2 tablespoons plus 2 teaspoons minced garlic
1 teaspoon salt
2 teaspoons ground black pepper
1 tablespoon cornstarch
1 tablespoon water
¼ cup oil
2 teaspoons fresh minced ginger
1 teaspoon bean sauce
1 cup red wine
½ cup catsup
5 tablespoons sugar
2 tablespoons fish sauce
Oil for deep-frying
3 sprigs of coriander

In a large bowl coat the chicken wings with 2 tablespoons of the garlic, salt, and black pepper. Allow to stand for ½ hour or longer.

Combine the cornstarch and water and set aside.

To make the sauce, in a medium saucepan heat the oil over high heat. When oil is hot, add 2 teaspoons of the garlic, ginger, and bean sauce. Sauté until the garlic is light brown. Add the red wine, catsup, sugar, fish sauce, and cornstarch mixture. Bring to a boil, reduce the heat to low, and simmer for 20 to 25 minutes, stirring occasionally. Remove from the stove and allow to cool to room temperature.

In a steamer, steam the chicken wings for 15 to 20 minutes, until its juices run clear when pierced. Remove and allow to cool.

In a deep-fryer, heat the oil to 400°. Deep-fry the chicken wings for 5 minutes, until they are browned and crisp. Drain on paper towels.

Place several chicken wings at a time into the sauce and coat thoroughly. Transfer to a serving platter. Repeat for the remaining chicken wings. Garnish with the coriander and serve.

Serves 4 to 6.

Seafood

PRAWNS WITH SPICY CHILI OIL
(Gung Pat Nam Prik Paow)

Prawns with Spicy Chili Oil is very popular at Siam Cuisine. If the Spicy Chili Oil has previously been made, this medium-hot dish is very quick and easy to make.

> 12 to 14 medium prawns, shelled and deveined (approximately 8 ounces)
> 4 ounces bamboo shoots, sliced into 10 to 12 wedges about ½ by 3 inches
> 8 medium button mushrooms, sliced
> 1½ tablespoons oil
> ½ teaspoon fish sauce
> 5 tablespoons Spicy Chili Oil (page 89)
> 3 green onions, cut into 2-inch lengths

Using a large strainer to hold the prawns, parboil for 3 seconds, until they turn pink on the edges. Be careful not to overcook; the cooking process will be completed later. Drain well and set aside.

Place the bamboo shoots and mushrooms in a well-seasoned pan or wok. Heat the pan over high heat without any oil, to remove the excess liquid.

Add the oil to the pan. When oil is hot, add the prawns and pour the fish sauce over them. Stir-fry for several seconds. Quickly add the Spicy Chili Oil and green onions. Stir-fry for about 2 minutes, until done. Serve immediately.

Serves 4.

PRAWNS AND CALAMARI IN SPICY CHILI OIL
(Gung Bla Murk Pat Nam Prik Paow)

Prawns and Calamari in Spicy Chili Oil is a medium-hot dish that is very similar to Prawns with Spicy Chili Oil.

8 medium prawns, shelled and deveined (approximately 5 ounces)

3 medium calamari (approximately 5 to 7 ounces)

4 ounces bamboo shoots, sliced into 10 to 12 wedges about ½ by 3 inches

8 medium button mushrooms, sliced medium thick

1½ tablespoons oil

½ teaspoon fish sauce

5 tablespoons Spicy Chili Oil (page 89)

3 green onions, cut into 2-inch lengths

Using a large strainer to hold the prawns, parboil for 3 seconds until they turn pink on the edges. Be careful not to overcook; the cooking process will be completed later. Drain well and set aside.

Clean the calamari (page 18) and slice the bodies into 1-inch rings. Place rings and tentacles in the strainer and parboil for 5 seconds, just until the meat becomes opaque and firms up. Be careful not to overcook; the calamari will become tough and chewy. Drain well and set aside.

Place the bamboo shoots and mushrooms in a well-seasoned pan or wok. Heat the pan over high heat without any oil, to remove the excess liquid.

Add the oil to the pan. When oil is hot, add the prawns and pour the fish sauce over them. Stir-fry for several seconds. Quickly add the Spicy Chili Oil and green onions. Stir-fry for about 2 minutes, until the prawns are almost done. Add the calamari and stir-fry for another 6 seconds. Serve immediately.

Serves 4.

 ## PRAWNS AND CALAMARI WITH SWEET BASIL
(Gung Bla Murk Pat Pet)

In Thailand, sweet basil dishes are served spicy hot. They use the fiery Thai chili peppers, pounded in a mortar with garlic and white peppercorns. These recipes call for jalapeño chili peppers; if you want it hotter, use Thai chili peppers instead.

2 dried cayenne peppers

6 medium prawns, shelled and deveined (approximately 4 ounces)

3 medium calamari (approximately 5 to 7 ounces)

1 tablespoon oil

1 teaspoon minced garlic

4 ounces bamboo shoots, sliced into 10 to 12 wedges about ¾ by 3 inches

Pinch of ground white pepper

3 jalapeño or serrano chili peppers, stems removed, cut length-wise into quarters

2 green onions, cut into 2-inch lengths

2 tablespoons oyster sauce

⅛ teaspoon sugar

1 cup fresh holy basil leaves, loosely packed *or* 25 to 35 orange mint or orange bergamot mint leaves

Soak the cayenne peppers in hot tap water for about 15 minutes, until soft. Drain and chop into small pieces. Reserve ½ teaspoon and set aside.

Using a large strainer to hold the prawns, parboil for 3 seconds until they turn pink on the edges. Be careful not to overcook; the cooking process will be completed later. Drain well and set aside.

Clean the calamari (page 18) and slice the bodies into 1-inch rings. Place the rings and tentacles in the strainer and parboil for 5 seconds, just until the meat becomes opaque and firms up. Be careful not to overcook or the calamari will become tough and chewy. Drain well and set aside.

Heat a well-seasoned pan or wok over high heat and add the oil. When oil is hot, add the garlic and cayenne peppers. Stir-fry until the garlic turns light brown.

Add the prawns, bamboo shoots, white pepper, and chili peppers. Stir-fry for several seconds. Add the green onions, oyster sauce, and sugar. Stir-fry for about 2 minutes, until the prawns are almost done. Add the calamari and holy basil leaves. Stir-fry for another 10 seconds. Serve immediately.

Serves 4.

PRAWNS AND SCALLOPS WITH SWEET BASIL
(Gung Scallops Pat Pet)

Prawns and Scallops with Sweet Basil is a very popular hot dish. If available, use holy basil leaves. At Siam Cuisine, orange bergamot mint leaves are substituted, giving this dish a distinctive flavor.

> 2 dried cayenne peppers
> 6 medium prawns, shelled and deveined (approximately 4 ounces)
> 6 large scallops (approximately 6 to 7 ounces)
> 1 tablespoon oil
> 1 teaspoon minced garlic
> 4 ounces bamboo shoots, sliced into 10 to 12 wedges about ¾ by 3 inches.
> Pinch of ground white pepper
> 3 jalapeño or serrano chili peppers, stems removed, cut lengthwise into quarters
> 2 green onions, cut into 2-inch lengths
> 2 tablespoons oyster sauce
> ⅛ teaspoon sugar
> 1 cup fresh holy basil leaves, loosely packed *or* 25 to 30 orange mint or orange bergamot mint leaves

Soak the cayenne peppers in hot tap water for about 15 minutes until soft. Drain and chop into small pieces. Reserve ½ teaspoon, and set aside.

Using a large strainer to hold the prawns, parboil for 3 seconds until they turn pink on the edges. Be careful not to overcook; the cooking process will be completed later. Drain well and set aside.

Place the scallops in the strainer and parboil for 2 to 3 seconds. Drain well and set aside.

Heat a well-seasoned pan or wok over high heat and add the oil. When oil is hot, add the garlic and cayenne peppers. Stir-fry until garlic turns light brown, being careful not to let it burn.

Add the prawns, scallops, bamboo shoots, white pepper, and chili peppers. Stir-fry for several seconds. Add the green onions, oyster sauce, and sugar. Stir-fry for 1½ minutes, until the prawns and scallops are almost done. Add the basil leaves and stir-fry for another 10 seconds, until the leaves are wilted. Serve immediately.

Serves 4.

 SCALLOPS WITH SWEET BASIL
(Scallops Pat Pet)

Scallops with Sweet Basil is hot and is very easy to prepare.

2 dried cayenne peppers
9 large scallops (approximately 10 ounces)
1 tablespoon oil
1 teaspoon minced garlic
4 ounces bamboo shoots, sliced into 10 to 12 wedges about ¾
    by 3 inches
Pinch of ground white pepper
3 jalapeño or serrano chili peppers, stems removed, cut
    lengthwise into quarters
2 green onions, cut into 2-inch lengths
2 tablespoons oyster sauce
⅛ teaspoon sugar
1 cup fresh holy basil leaves, loosely packed *or* 25 to 35 orange
    mint or orange bergamot mint leaves

Soak the cayenne peppers in hot water for about 15 minutes, until soft.
    Drain and chop into small pieces. Reserve ½ teaspoon and set aside.
Using a large strainer to hold the scallops, parboil for 3 seconds. Drain
    well and set aside.
Heat a well-seasoned pan or wok over high heat and add the oil. When
    oil is hot, add the garlic and cayenne peppers. Stir-fry until the garlic
    turns light brown, being careful not to let it burn.
Add the scallops, bamboo shoots, white pepper, and chili peppers. Stir-
    fry for several seconds. Add the green onions, oyster sauce, and
    sugar. Stir-fry for 2 minutes, until the scallops are almost done. Add
    the basil leaves and stir-fry for another 10 seconds, until the leaves
    are wilted. Serve immediately.

Serves 4.

CALAMARI WITH SWEET BASIL
(Bla Murk Pat Pet)

This dish is hot, but it can be adjusted according to your taste. For a real delicacy, Somchai likes to cook Calamari with Sweet Basil using only the tentacles.

> 2 dried cayenne peppers
> 6 large calamari (approximately 12 to 14 ounces)
> 1 tablespoon oil
> 1 teaspoon minced garlic
> Pinch of ground white pepper
> 3 jalapeño or serrano chili peppers, stems removed, cut lengthwise into quarters
> 2 tablespoons oyster sauce
> ⅛ teaspoon sugar
> 2 green onions, cut into 2-inch lengths
> 1 cup fresh holy basil leaves, loosely packed *or* 25 to 35 orange mint or orange bergamot mint leaves

Soak the cayenne peppers in hot water for about 15 minutes, until soft. Drain and chop into small pieces. Reserve ½ teaspoon and set aside.

Clean the calamari (page 18) and slice the bodies into 1-inch rings. Using a large strainer to hold the calamari, parboil for 5 seconds, just until they become opaque and firm up. Be careful not to overcook. Drain well and set aside.

Heat a well-seasoned pan or wok over high heat and add the oil. When oil is hot, add the garlic and cayenne peppers. Stir-fry until the garlic turns light brown.

Proceeding quickly to avoid overcooking the calamari, add the calamari, white pepper, and chili peppers. Stir-fry for several seconds. Add the oyster sauce, sugar, and green onions. Stir-fry for 1 minute. Add the basil leaves and stir-fry for about 10 seconds, until the leaves are wilted. Serve immediately.

Serves 4.

CALAMARI WITH GINGER
(Bla Murk Pat King)

Calamari with Ginger has a mild sweet and sour flavor. To temper the sharpness of the ginger, cut it into fine julienne pieces.

¼ ounce small dried black fungus (cloud ears)
6 large calamari (approximately 14 to 16 ounces)
1½ tablespoons oil
1 tablespoon minced garlic
1 teaspoon bean sauce
2-inch section fresh ginger, peeled and sliced into fine julienne
     pieces (approximately 1½ ounces)
¼ medium yellow onion
Pinch of ground white pepper
4 tablespoons fresh Chicken Stock (page 53)
2 tablespoons oyster sauce
2 tablespoons Kwan's Sweet and Sour Sauce (page 87)
2 green onions, sliced into 2-inch lengths

Soak the black fungus in a small bowl of water for 5 to 10 minutes until soft. Drain well and set aside.

Clean the calamari (page 18), and slice the bodies into 1-inch rings. Using a large strainer to hold the rings and tentacles, parboil for 5 seconds, just until they become opaque and firm up. Be careful not to overcook or they will become tough and chewy. Drain well and set aside.

Heat a well-seasoned pan or wok over high heat and add the oil. When oil is hot, add the garlic, bean sauce, and ginger. Stir-fry until the garlic is light brown.

Add the black fungus, yellow onion, white pepper, and Chicken Stock. Stir-fry for 1 minute. Add the oyster sauce, sweet and sour sauce, and green onions. Stir-fry for another 30 seconds. Add the calamari and stir-fry for 15 seconds. Serve immediately.

Serves 4.

SCALLOPS WITH GINGER
(Scallops Pat King)

Scallops with Ginger is a mild dish and is easy to prepare.

¼ ounce small dried black fungus (cloud ears)
9 to 10 large scallops (approximately 10 to 12 ounces)
1½ tablespoons oil
1 tablespoon minced garlic
1 teaspoon bean sauce
2-inch section fresh ginger, peeled and sliced into fine julienne
    pieces (approximately 1½ ounces)
¼ medium yellow onion
Pinch of ground white pepper
2 tablespoons oyster sauce
2 tablespoons Kwan's Sweet and Sour Sauce (page 87)
2 tablespoons fresh Chicken Stock (page 53)
2 green onions, cut into 2-inch lengths

Soak the black fungus in a small bowl of water for 5 to 10 minutes until
    soft. Drain and set aside.
Using a large strainer to hold the scallops, parboil for 3 seconds. Drain
    well and set aside.
Heat a well-seasoned pan or wok over high heat and add the oil. When
    oil is hot, add the garlic, bean sauce, and ginger. Stir-fry until the
    garlic is light brown.
Add the black fungus, scallops, yellow onion, white pepper, and oyster
    sauce. Stir-fry for several seconds. Add the sweet and sour sauce,
    Chicken Stock, and green onions. Stir-fry for 2 to 3 minutes. Serve
    immediately.

Serves 4.

FRIED FISH WITH SPICY SAUCE
(Bla Tot Lat Prik)

Fried Fish with Spicy Sauce has a very pungent, hot sauce,
which is prepared separately and then poured over the fish. Thais like
their fried fish very crisp on the outside and well done inside. They leave

the head and fins intact and eat all parts, including the crunchy fins, tail, and small bones.

 ½ cup oil
 Red Curry Paste II (page 82)
 1 tablespoon dried shrimp, ground in a blender
 ¼ teaspoon salt
 2 tablespoons sugar
 ⅓ teaspoon shrimp paste
 7 tablespoons fish sauce
 ¼ to 1 cup fresh Chicken Stock (page 53)
 2- to 2½-pound whole rock cod or other firm-fleshed fish, cleaned
 Oil for frying
 30 Thai or Italian basil leaves
 3 whole Kaffir lime leaves, sliced into fine slivers
 1 jalapeño or serrano chili pepper, stem removed, cut lengthwise into quarters

Heat a well-seasoned pan or wok over high heat and add the oil. When the oil is hot, add the curry paste, ground shrimp, salt, sugar, shrimp paste, and fish sauce. Reduce over high heat for about 10 minutes, until red-colored oil surfaces. Stir as needed to prevent sticking or burning. Lower the heat to medium and cook for another 20 minutes. If the sauce gets too dry and starts to stick, add ¼ cup of the Chicken Stock and mix well; repeat as necessary.

While the sauce is cooking, pat the rock cod dry with paper towels inside and out. Make three diagonal incisions, ¾ inch deep, on each side of the fish about 1½ inches apart. Set aside.

In a skillet large enough to hold the fish, heat 1 inch of oil over high heat until it starts to smoke. Holding the fish by the tail, lower it slowly into the hot oil. Starting at one edge of the skillet, slide the fish across the bottom. This will keep the splattering to a minimum. Fry the fish for 4 to 7 minutes on each side until crisp. (If you have a large deep-fryer that can hold the fish, deep-fry at 450° for 7 minutes, until done.) Drain on paper towels and place on a large serving platter. Set aside.

Remove the sauce from the stove and quickly add the basil and Kaffir lime leaves. Mix thoroughly. Pour the sauce over the fish, garnish with the chili pepper, and serve immediately.

 Serves 6.

FRESH BAKED FISH IN BANANA LEAF
(Bla Bing)

Fish prepared in this manner bakes in its own juices and comes out tender and moist, absorbing the flavors of the lemon grass and Thai basil. This dish is very easy to prepare and is wonderful at an outdoor barbecue. Before grilling the fish, make sure the aluminum foil is tightly sealed to prevent the steam from escaping. This will ensure that the fish is thoroughly cooked.

> 2½-pound whole rock cod or other firm-fleshed fish, cleaned
> 4 stalks fresh lemon grass, crushed
> Heavy-duty aluminum foil
> 1 fresh banana leaf, rinsed and wiped dry
> 3 medium yellow onions, sliced
> 4 green onions, cut into 3-inch lengths
> 50 Thai or Italian basil leaves

Make 3 to 4 diagonal incisions, ¾ inch deep, on each side of the fish about 1½ inches apart. Fold 2 stalks of the lemon grass in half and stuff them through the mouth of the fish into the body cavity.

Cut a piece of aluminum foil about 46 inches long, and fold in half so that it is 23 by 18 inches. Place it on a flat surface. Cut a piece of banana leaf approximately 15 by 20 inches. Place it in the center of the foil with the 15-inch edge parallel to the 23-inch edge of the foil.

In the center of the banana leaf layer the following ingredients in order across the 15-inch length: ½ of the yellow onions, ½ of the green onions, ½ of the Thai basil leaves, and 1 stalk of the lemon grass, cut into 4-inch lengths. Place the rock cod on top. Reverse the order of the ingredients and layer over the fish. (Add more basil and lemon grass, if desired, for more aroma and flavor.)

To wrap the fish, bring up the 15-inch edges of the banana leaf and overlap. Bring up the 23-inch edges of the aluminum foil and roll them tightly together. Seal the ends of the foil by twisting tightly. Remove as much air as possible from inside the foil before sealing.

Light a charcoal grill to an even, high heat. Adjust the grill to 3 to 4 inches above the coals. Grill the fish until done, 7 to 8 minutes on each side. Remove from the grill and place on a serving platter.

When ready to eat, cut the foil and banana leaf with the edge of a fork. Serve with Thai Barbecued Chicken Sauce (page 89) or Green Chili Sauce (page 87).

Serves 4 to 6.

FRIED FISH WITH SWEET AND SOUR GRAVY
(Bla Saum Roat)

The mild sauce for this fish is very quick and easy to make. Fry the fish just before serving, and then prepare the sauce. This means you will have to prepare all the ingredients in advance so there will be no delays once the fish has been fried.

1 tablespoon cornstarch
3 tablespoons water
2½-pound whole rock cod or other firm-fleshed fish, cleaned
Oil for frying
3 tablespoons oil
2-inch section fresh ginger, peeled and sliced into fine julienne
    pieces
2 teaspoons minced garlic
¼ teaspoon ground white pepper
2 teaspoons bean sauce
1 cup fresh Chicken Stock (page 53)
½ teaspoon sugar
1 tablespoon Kwan's Sweet and Sour Sauce (page 87)
¼ teaspoon sweet soy sauce
7 teaspoons oyster sauce
4 green onions, cut into 2-inch lengths
¼ teaspoon sesame oil
⅓ cup fresh coriander leaves

Combine the cornstarch and water in a small bowl and set aside.

Pat the rock cod dry inside and out with paper towels. Make 3 to 4 diagonal incisions, ¾ inch deep, on each side of the fish about 1½ inches apart. Set aside.

In a skillet large enough to hold the fish, heat 1 inch of oil over high heat until it starts to smoke. Holding the fish by the tail, lower it slowly into the hot oil. Starting at one edge of the skillet, slide the fish across the bottom. This will keep the splattering to a minimum. Fry the fish for 5 to 7 minutes on each side, until crisp. (If you have a large deep-fryer that can hold the fish, deep-fry at 450° for 7 minutes, until done.) Drain on paper towels and place on a large serving platter. Set aside.

Heat a well-seasoned pan over medium-high heat and add 3 tablespoons of oil. When oil is hot, add the ginger, garlic, and white pepper.

Stir-fry until the garlic turns light brown.

Add the bean sauce, Chicken Stock, sugar, sweet and sour sauce, sweet soy sauce, oyster sauce, cornstarch mixture, and green onions. Stir-fry for 2 minutes. Turn off the heat and add the sesame oil.

Top the fish with coriander and pour the sauce over it. Serve immediately.

Serves 4 to 6.

FRIED FILET OF FISH
(Bla Jean)

These fried filets are smothered in a very hot jalapeño chili pepper sauce. Despite the "heat," the aroma and flavor do come through. You may want to serve the sauce in a small bowl along with a bowl of Lime Sauce (page 93) for those who prefer something milder. Small, whole fish may be substituted and fried until crisp. The Thai people like to eat it bones and all.

⅛ cup sliced garlic
1 cup sliced shallots
4 green jalapeño or serrano chili peppers, stems removed
4 red jalapeño chili peppers, stems removed
½ cup water
½ cup oil
1 teaspoon salt
8 teaspoons sugar
1 tablespoon fish sauce
3 tablespoons Golden Mountain sauce
3 whole Kaffir lime leaves, sliced into fine slivers
2 rock cod filets, 1 inch thick, 10 to 12 ounces each or other firm-fleshed fish filets
⅓ cup rice flour
Oil for frying
30 Thai or Italian basil leaves

Place the garlic, shallots, chili peppers, and water in a blender; chop at very low speed into small pieces. Do not grind to a paste. Set aside.

Heat a well-seasoned pan or wok over medium heat and add the ½ cup of oil. When oil is hot, add the contents of the blender, salt, sugar, fish sauce, and Golden Mountain Sauce. Bring to a boil and reduce

for 20 minutes. Stir to prevent sticking. Add the Kaffir limes leaves
and cook another 5 to 10 minutes.

While the sauce cooks, cut the filets into pieces 1 inch wide, holding the
knife at an angle. Pat each piece dry with a paper towel and roll in
rice flour to lightly coat.

In a skillet large enough to hold the fish, heat 1 inch of oil over high heat
until it starts to smoke. Add the fish and fry for 5 minutes, until
golden brown. Drain and arrange on a serving platter.

Remove the sauce from the heat and add the Thai basil leaves. Stir and
pour over the fish. Serve immediately.

Serves 4 to 6.

 ## SIAM SPECIAL
(Boy Sien)

Siam Special combines a wide variety of ingredients in a mild
sauce and is easy to prepare.

> 4 medium prawns, shelled and deveined (approximately 2½
>   ounces)
> 2 medium calamari (approximately 3 to 5 ounces)
> 1¾ teaspoons cornstarch
> 1 tablespoon water
> 1 tablespoon oil
> 1 tablespoon minced garlic
> 1½ ounces fried fish cake or fish balls, sliced into several pieces
> 10-ounce can *sze hsien kow fu* (chop suey vegetables), liquid
>   reserved
> 3 baby corn, cut in half lengthwise
> 2 green onions, cut into 2-inch lengths
> 2 tablespoons fresh Chicken Stock (page 53)
> 1½ teaspoons oyster sauce
> ½ teaspoon sesame oil

Using a large strainer to hold the prawns, parboil for 3 seconds until they
turn pink on the edges. Be careful not to overcook; the cooking
process will be completed later. Drain and set aside.

Clean the calamari (page 18), and slice the bodies into 1-inch rings. Place
the rings and tentacles in the strainer; parboil for 5 seconds, until

they become opaque and firm up. Be careful not to overcook or the calamari will become tough and chewy. Drain and set aside.

Combine the cornstarch and water, reserve 1 tablespoon, and set aside.

Heat a well-seasoned pan or wok over high heat and add the oil. When oil is hot, add the garlic and stir-fry until light brown.

Add the prawns, fish cake, *sze hsien kow fu* with its liquid, baby corn, green onions, Chicken Stock, oyster sauce, and cornstarch mixture. Stir-fry for about 1½ minutes. Add the calamari and stir-fry for a few seconds. Remove from heat and pour the sesame oil on top. Serve immediately.

Serves 4.

IMPERIAL PRAWNS
(Gung Pat Kana)

Imperial Prawns is very easy to make and combines broccoli and prawns in a mild sauce.

    8 ounces broccoli
    8 to 10 medium prawns, shelled and deveined (approximately
        5 to 7 ounces)
    3½ teaspoons cornstarch
    2 tablespoons water
    1½ tablespoons oil
    1 tablespoon minced garlic
    ½ tablespoon bean sauce
    ⅛ teaspoon ground white pepper
    ½ cup fresh Chicken Stock (page 53)
    3 tablespoons oyster sauce
    ½ teaspoon sweet soy sauce
    1 tablespoon Kwan's Sweet and Sour Sauce (page 87)
    ½ teaspoon white vinegar
    ½ teaspoon sesame oil

To prepare the broccoli, cut the flowers 2½ inches from the top and separate into smaller sections. Peel the stem and cut into rectangular pieces about 3 by 1¼ by ³⁄₁₆ inches. Blanch the broccoli for about 10 seconds. Drain and set aside.

Using a large strainer to hold the prawns, parboil for 3 seconds until they turn pink on the edges. Be careful not to overcook; the cooking process will be completed later. Drain well and set aside.

Combine the cornstarch and water in a small bowl. Reserve 1½ tablespoons and set aside.

Heat a well-seasoned pan or wok over high heat and add the oil. When oil is hot, add the garlic, bean sauce, and white pepper. Stir-fry until the garlic is light brown.

Add the Chicken Stock and oyster sauce and bring to a boil. Add the broccoli and stir-fry for 10 to 15 seconds. Add the cornstarch mixture and the prawns and stir-fry for 30 seconds. Add the sweet soy sauce, sweet and sour sauce, and white vinegar; stir-fry for another 30 seconds, until the prawns are done. Remove from heat and pour the sesame oil on top. Serve immediately.

Serves 4.

 ## JUMBO PRAWNS
(Gung Nang)

To celebrate Garlic Week in Berkeley, Somchai and Kwan served these Jumbo Prawns, which are loaded with garlic. Use forks to remove the prawns from their shells at the table. Serve with Thai Barbecued Chicken Sauce (page 89) and enjoy!

6 jumbo fresh water prawns (4 to 6 per pound)
3 tablespoons garlic, crushed and minced
1 tablespoon ground white pepper
1 teaspoon fish sauce
1 egg, lightly beaten
1 tablespoon finely grated bread crumbs
Oil for deep-frying

Butterfly and devein the prawns, but do not shell them. Lay them open flat and set aside.

In a small mixing bowl combine the garlic, white pepper, and fish sauce.

Evenly coat the cut surface of each prawn with 1½ teaspoons of the garlic mixture. Dip the same surface in the beaten egg and lightly sprinkle with ½ teaspoon of the bread crumbs. Shake off any excess and set aside.

In a deep-fryer, heat the oil to 380°. Deep-fry several prawns at a time for 2 minutes, until coated side is golden brown, turning occasionally. Remove from the oil and drain on paper towels. Repeat for the remaining prawns. Serve immediately with Thai Barbecued Chicken Sauce (page 89).

Serves 4.

GARLIC MACKEREL
(Bla Tu)

This recipe is another garlic specialty served during Garlic Week in Berkeley. Mackerel is very oily and many people consider it fishy-tasting, but the garlic seems to overshadow the strong flavor. In this recipe the fish is both baked and grilled, keeping it moist and tender. Two tablespoons of soft butter may be substituted for the garlic salt and oil, if you prefer.

    2 Spanish mackerels, 1 pound each
    4 teaspoons garlic, crushed and minced
    1 teaspoon ground white pepper
    ¼ teaspoon garlic salt
    2 tablespoons vegetable oil

Filet the mackerel, leaving the skin intact, or have your fishmonger do it. Place the 4 filets in a baking pan, skin-side down. Set aside.

In a small bowl combine the garlic, white pepper, garlic salt, and oil.

Evenly coat the cut surface of each filet with ¼ of the mixture. Allow to stand for at least 1 hour in the refrigerator.

Preheat the oven to 550°. Bake the filets for 5 minutes, until the garlic has turned brown on the edges. Remove and set aside.

Light a charcoal grill to an even, medium-high heat. Adjust the grill to 3 to 4 inches above the coals. Grill the mackerel, skin-side down, for 2 to 3 minutes, until grill marks show on the skin. Serve with Thai Barbecued Chicken Sauce (page 89) and/or Lime Sauce (page 93).

Serves 4 to 6.

CRAB DELIGHT
(Gung Bu Pat Pong Garee)

This crab dish uses just enough yellow curry powder to give it a slight tang. It may appear that the amount of oil called for is incorrect. However, this dish becomes gooey and sticks to the pan if less oil is used. If the snow crab is frozen, defrost it completely before using. Taste the crab before cooking to check its salt content and adjust the amount of fish sauce accordingly. Do not stir or flip the ingredients too much; the crab meat tends to fall apart.

> 7 medium prawns, shelled and deveined (approximately 4½ ounces)
> ½ teaspoon cornstarch
> 1 teaspoon water
> 4 tablespoons oil
> 1 tablespoon minced garlic
> ¼ medium yellow onion
> Pinch of ground white pepper
> ¾ teaspoon yellow curry powder
> 3 ounces snow crab meat
> 3 ounces snow crab leg meat
> 2½ ounces bamboo shoots, sliced into 6 wedges about ½ by 3 inches
> 1 teaspoon fish sauce
> ¾ teaspoon sugar
> 1 green onion, cut into 2-inch lengths

Using a large strainer to hold the prawns, parboil for 3 seconds until they turn pink on the edges. Be careful not to overcook; the cooking process will be completed later. Drain and set aside.

In a small bowl combine the cornstarch and water and set aside.

Heat a well-seasoned pan or wok over high heat and add the oil. When oil is hot, add the garlic, yellow onion, white pepper, and curry powder in order. Stir-fry until the garlic is light brown.

Add the snow crab and bamboo shoots. Stir carefully, completely coating the crab with the curry mixture. Add the prawns and pour the fish sauce over them. Add the cornstarch mixture and sugar and stir-fry for 30 seconds. Add the green onions and stir-fry for another 30 seconds, until the prawns are done. Serve immediately.

Serves 4.

RED CURRY FISH
(Gang Shu Shi Bla)

In Thailand it is customary to make this recipe with fresh-water fish, but Kwan likes to use rock cod filets. Red Curry Fish is medium hot. The amount of ground cayenne pepper can be adjusted according to your taste, but to achieve the proper flavor don't eliminate it completely.

> 1 pound rock cod filet or other firm-fleshed fish filet
> 5 tablespoons Basic Curry Paste (page 79)
> 1 to 1½ tablespoons ground cayenne pepper
> 2½ cups thick coconut milk
> 4 tablespoons fish sauce
> 2 tablespoons sugar
> ½ to 1 cup fresh Chicken Stock (page 53)
> 1 green and 1 red jalapeño chili pepper, cut lengthwise into
>   quarters
> ½ cup Thai or Italian basil leaves (approximately 30 leaves)

Holding the knife at an angle, cut the rock cod filet into pieces 3 inches wide. Set aside.

Combine the curry paste, ground cayenne pepper, 1¼ cups of the coconut milk, fish sauce, and sugar in a large well-seasoned pan or wok. Bring to a boil over high heat. Reduce the curry for 7 to 10 minutes, until the mixture becomes dry and pasty. Scrape the sides and bottom of the pan as needed to prevent sticking or burning.

Tiny pockets of oil from the coconut milk should start to surface at this time. If the oil does not surface, add 3 to 4 tablespoons of the Chicken Stock and bring to a boil. Reduce for 4 to 5 minutes. Repeat if necessary.

Add ½ cup of the Chicken Stock and the remaining 1¼ cups of coconut milk. Bring to a boil over high heat. Add the fish. Cover and boil for 6 to 7 minutes, until the fish is done. Turn off the heat and add the chili peppers and basil leaves. Stir lightly and serve immediately.

Serves 4.

GREEN CURRY FISH WITH KRACHAI
(Gang Keow Waan Bla Krachai)

Green Curry Fish with Krachai is very hot. It is similar in many ways to Green Curry Pork, but the *krachai* gives it a totally different flavor. In Thailand, catfish is often used in this curry; this recipe calls for trout. If fresh or frozen *krachai* is not available, sliced *krachai* in a jar may be substituted.

> 1 trout, about 12 ounces
> Green Curry Paste (page 80)
> 1½ teaspoons sugar
> 3 tablespoons fish sauce
> 2½ cups thick coconut milk
> 1¾ cups fresh Chicken Stock (page 53)
> 2 ounces fresh or frozen *krachai* (page 28), sliced into julienne pieces (approximately ½ cup)
> 30 Thai or Italian basil leaves
> 1 jalapeño or serrano chili pepper, stem removed, cut lengthwise into quarters

Clean the trout, removing the fins. Make 2 or 3 diagonal slices, ¼ inch deep, on each side of the fish about 1½ inches apart. Set aside.

To a large, well-seasoned pan or wok, add the Green Curry Paste, sugar, fish sauce, and 1 cup of the coconut milk. Bring to a boil and reduce over high heat for 15 to 25 minutes. Scrape the sides and bottom of the pan as needed to prevent sticking or burning, as the mixture becomes dry and pasty.

Tiny pockets of oil from the coconut milk should start to surface at this time. If the oil does not surface, add 3 to 4 tablespoons of the Chicken Stock and bring to a boil. Reduce for 4 to 5 minutes. Repeat if necessary.

Cook for another 10 to 15 minutes at medium-high heat. Scrape the sides and bottom of the pan.

Add the remaining 1½ cups of coconut milk and 1 cup of the Chicken Stock; bring to a boil. Add the trout and *krachai*. Boil over medium-high heat for 7 to 10 minutes, until the trout is just done. Do not stir. Add ¼ cup of the Chicken Stock if it gets too dry. Remove from the stove and add the Thai basil leaves, stirring carefully until the leaves are wilted. Garnish with the chili pepper and serve immediately.

Serves 4 to 6.

STEAMED FISH CURRY IN BANANA-LEAF BOWL (*Haw Mok Bla*)

This fish mousse, which is steamed over vegetables in a banana-leaf bowl, possesses an extraordinary blend of spices. The medium-hot red curry paste used in this recipe should be very dry. Since pounding the ingredients creates a lot of excess liquid, Kwan has added an extra step to remove the liquid, keeping the paste at the proper consistency. This recipe makes 8 banana leaf bowls, each serving anywhere from 1 to 4 people. That may sound like a lot, but, if cooked and properly sealed, each "bowl" can be stored in the refrigerator for 2 days, or in the freezer for up to 2 months. Bring to room temperature before reheating in a steamer for about 5 minutes.

> Red Curry Paste III (page 83)
> 5 cups coconut cream
> 1 large or 2 small eggs
> 1 pound ground fish (page 25)
> 2 pounds rock cod filet or other firm-fleshed fish filet
> 3 large banana leaves, rinsed and wiped dry
> 32 round toothpicks or bamboo slivers
> 2 cups Thai or Italian basil leaves, firmly packed *or* 2 bunches
>   spinach *or* 1 small napa cabbage
> 4 to 5 whole Kaffir lime leaves, fresh or frozen, sliced into fine
>   slivers
> 8 sprigs fresh coriander
> 1 red jalapeño chili pepper, seeded and sliced lengthwise into
>   slivers

To remove the liquid from the red curry paste, reduce it in a well-seasoned pan over medium-low heat until it is sticky and heavy and retains its shape. Scrape the sides and bottom of the pan constantly so that the paste does not stick or burn. Remove from heat and transfer to a large bowl. Set aside.

Reserve ¾ cup of the coconut cream to use later as the topping.

Add the remaining coconut cream, egg, and ground fish to the curry paste. Combine and set aside.

Pat the filets dry with paper towels. Slice them into 2-inch squares and add to the curry paste mixture. Stir, "bruising" the fish with the edge of the spoon so it will absorb the curry paste. Set aside.

To make the banana-leaf bowls, cut the leaves into 16 circles, each 8 inches in diameter. Use an 8-inch plate as a template. Place 2 circles together. Bring up the edges and make 4 pleats, equal distance apart, to form a bowl 2 inches deep. Attach each pleat to the bowl with a toothpick. Repeat, making 8 bowls.

Divide the basil leaves or other vegetable (see below) into 8 equal portions. Place one portion in the bottom of each banana-leaf bowl. Fill each bowl with ⅛ of the curry paste mixture, making sure there is an equal amount of fish filet in each. Smooth out the surface.

Top each bowl with 1½ tablespoons of the reserved coconut cream. Garnish with ⅛ of the slivered Kaffir lime leaf, 1 sprig of fresh coriander, and several slivers of chili pepper.

Place a banana-leaf bowl on a heat-resistant plate and steam for 20 minutes over medium-high heat. Remove and repeat for the remaining 7 bowls.

Makes 8.

If spinach or napa cabbage is used, clean and drain. Parboil for a few seconds, until the leaves are wilted. Run under cold water to stop the cooking process. Squeeze out any excess liquid. Slice into 2-inch pieces. (Do not parboil the basil leaves.)

PINEAPPLE CURRY
(Gang Kua Saparot Gung)

Pineapple Curry is a medium-hot curry with a tart taste that comes from fresh pineapple. It is important to extract just enough of the pineapple's juice so that the curry does not taste soapy.

> 1 fresh pineapple, 3½ to 4 pounds
> 15 mussels, cleaned and debearded
> 2 tablespoons large dried shrimp (approximately ½ ounce)
> Red Curry Paste IV (page 84)
> 1½ teaspoons sugar
> 3 tablespoons fish sauce
> 3½ cups thick coconut milk
> 1½ to 2 cups fresh Chicken Stock (page 53)
> 1 pound medium prawns, shelled and deveined

To prepare the pineapple, cut off the top and remove the rind and eyes. Coarsely chop the pineapple and place in a large bowl. Discard the core. Gently knead the chopped pineapple until about 1 cup of the juice is released. Use a large strainer to drain and discard the juice. Set the chopped pineapple aside.

Parboil the mussels for 3 minutes, until they open and the meat pulls away from the shell. Drain. Remove the meat and discard the shells. Set the meat aside.

In a mortar pound the dried shrimp into flat, soft, crumbly pieces. Set aside.

Combine the curry paste, sugar, fish sauce, dried shrimp, and 1 cup of the coconut milk in a large, well-seasoned pan or wok. Bring to a boil over high heat. Lower the heat to medium high and reduce the curry for 25 minutes, until it becomes dry and pasty. Scrape the sides and bottom of the pan as needed to prevent sticking or burning. Add 1 cup of the coconut milk. Stir and reduce for another 10 to 15 minutes.

Tiny pockets of oil from the coconut milk should start to surface at this time. If the oil does not surface, add 3 to 4 tablespoons of the Chicken Stock and bring to a boil. Reduce for 4 to 5 minutes. Repeat if necessary.

Cook for another 10 minutes at medium-high heat. Add the remaining 1½ cups of coconut milk and 1½ cups of Chicken Stock. Stir and bring to a boil. Add the pineapple and bring to a boil again. Add the prawns and mussels and turn off heat. Serve immediately.

Serves 8.

 FISH IN TAMARIND SAUCE
(Bla Thom Som)

In Thailand, whole fresh-water fish is ordinarily used for this dish; however, rock cod may be substituted. The fish is cooked in a broth containing tamarind, giving it a mouth-watering tanginess. Fresh and dried chili peppers are added for hotness and extra fragrance. Never reheat this dish; it must be served immediately.

3 ounces preserved tamarind
¾ cup hot water
1 trout, cleaned (12 to 16 ounces)
2-inch section fresh ginger (approximately 1½ ounces)
1 stalk lemon grass
25 white peppercorns *or* ½ teaspoon ground white pepper
2 fresh coriander plants, lightly chopped (save the roots)
½ teaspoon salt
2 medium shallots, peeled (approximately 2½ ounces)
1 teaspoon shrimp paste
2 cups fresh Chicken Stock (page 53)
4 teaspoons palm sugar
2 tablespoons fish sauce
4 dried red chili peppers, 2 to 3 inches long, or dried cayenne
   peppers
5 to 6 red and green jalapeño chili peppers
2 green onions, cut into 1½-inch lengths

In a small bowl soak the tamarind in the hot water for 30 minutes, until soft. Work the tamarind with your hands for 10 minutes to release the pulp. Press pulp through a strainer. Squeeze out all the liquid and pulp and discard the twigs and seeds. Reserve 6 tablespoons and set aside.

Make 3 diagonal incisions, ¼ inch deep, on each side of the trout about 1½ inches apart. Set aside.

Peel ⅓ of the ginger and slice into fine julienne pieces. Smash the remainder with the side of a cleaver. Set aside.

Thinly slice 1 teaspoon of the lemon grass. Place in a mortar and set aside. Crush the remaining stalk with the end of a cleaver. Fold into thirds and tie together with one of the loose stems of lemon grass. Set aside.

Add the white peppercorns, coriander roots, and salt to the mortar, and pound into a paste. Gradually add the shallots and pound into small pieces. Add the shrimp paste and pound until dissolved. Add 1 teaspoon of water if necessary.

Transfer the ingredients to a saucepan large enough to hold the fish. (It is best if the fish is completely covered by the sauce, but it is not necessary.) Add the Chicken Stock, smashed ginger, and folded lemon grass. Bring to a boil over high heat. Add the tamarind, palm sugar, fish sauce, dried chili peppers, and trout. Cover and boil for 3 minutes. Sprinkle the julienned ginger over the fish and cook for 7 minutes, until the fish is done. Turn off the heat and add the chili peppers, green onions, and chopped coriander. Cover and allow to stand for about 2 minutes before serving.

Serves 4.

STEAMED FISH
(Bla Nurng)

This recipe is similar to one version of Chinese steamed fish. The flavors are mild, and it is very simple to make. Use either fresh-water or salt-water fish.

> 2-pound whole rock cod or black bass, cleaned
> 5-ounce can salted lettuce, thinly sliced (save brine)
> 3 tablespoons Golden Mountain sauce
> 1½ tablespoons sesame oil
> 1 teaspoon sweet soy sauce
> 1 teaspoon bean sauce
> 1 tablespoon sugar
> ½ teaspoon ground white pepper
> 1½-inch section fresh ginger, peeled and sliced into fine julienne pieces (approximately 1 ounce)
> 2 large green onions, thinly sliced diagonally
> 1 cup Chinese celery, sliced into 1-inch lengths, loosely packed

Pat the rock cod dry with paper towels inside and out. Make 3 diagonal incisions, ¾ inch deep, on each side of the fish about 1½ inches apart. Place on a platter that will fit in your steamer. Set aside.

In a small bowl combine the brine from the salted lettuce, Golden Mountain sauce, sesame oil, sweet soy sauce, bean sauce, sugar, and white pepper. Pour over the fish, coating both sides.

Sprinkle the salted lettuce, ginger, green onions, and Chinese celery over the fish.

Steam the fish for about 15 minutes, until just done. Serve immediately.

Serves 6.

SEAFOOD CLAY POT
(Bot Daek)

Seafood Clay Pot is a Thai bouillabaisse. It contains a variety of seafood and a rich broth, which is spiked with a spicy chili oil to give it a mouth-watering tanginess. It is medium hot and can be served with Green Chili Sauce (page 87).

> 2 cups fresh Chicken Stock (page 53)
> 7 teaspoons fish sauce
> 2 tablespoons Spicy Chili Oil for Hot and Sour Prawn Soup (page 90)
> 5 teaspoons fresh lime juice
> 1 stalk fresh lemon grass
> 1 to 3 jalapeño or serrano chili peppers, stems removed, crushed
> 2 whole Kaffir lime leaves
> 5 ounces rock cod filet or any firm-fleshed fish
> 6 or 7 mussels, cleaned and debearded
> 6 to 8 medium prawns, shelled and deveined (approximately 5 ounces)
> 2 medium calamari (approximately 3 to 5 ounces)
> 5 to 6 large scallops (approximately 5 ounces)
> 2 fresh or frozen snow crab legs
> ½ cup fresh coriander leaves, loosely packed

Soak a clay pot and its cover in water for 1 hour or overnight.

Place the Chicken Stock, fish sauce, Spicy Chili Oil, and 3 teaspoons of the fresh lime juice in the clay pot. Bring to a boil over high heat and cook until the oil is combined. Turn off the heat and set aside.

Cut the lemon grass in half lengthwise and then into 3-inch pieces. Crush with the end of a cleaver. Add the lemon grass, chili peppers, and Kaffir lime leaves to the clay pot.

Cut the rock cod filet into 3 pieces and place in the clay pot. Add the mussels and cover the pot. Set aside.

Using a strainer to hold the prawns, parboil for about 10 seconds. Drain and set aside.

Clean the calamari (page 18) and slice the bodies into 1-inch rings. Using the strainer to hold the rings and tentacles, parboil for 4 seconds, until they become opaque and firm up. Drain and set aside.

Using the strainer, parboil the scallops for 3 seconds. Drain and set aside.

Place the clay pot on the stove and bring to a boil over high heat. Boil, covered, for 3 minutes, or until the mussels open up and the meat starts to pull away from the shell.

Add the scallops and crab legs to the clay pot and cover. Boil for 30 seconds. Turn off the heat.

Add the prawns and calamari and top with the coriander and remaining lime juice. Cover and serve immediately.

Serves 4 to 6.

 ## MUSSEL CLAY POT
(Hoy Malang Phu Mar Din)

In this recipe the mussels are steamed in a chicken broth. They relinquish their juices, adding a richness to the mild liquid. This dish is very quick and easy to make, but be careful not to overcook it or the mussels will shrink and become very tough.

2 stalks fresh lemon grass, crushed and cut into 3-inch lengths
½ cup coarsely chopped shallots
6 tablespoons fresh Chicken Stock (page 53)
2 pounds mussels, cleaned and debearded
30 to 40 Thai or Italian basil leaves

Soak a clay pot and its cover in water for 1 hour or overnight.

Layer the lemon grass, shallots, Chicken Stock, and mussels in the clay pot in order. Cover the pot and bring to a boil over high heat. Cook for 3 to 5 minutes, until the mussels open and the meat starts to pull away from the shell. Add the basil; cover and turn off the heat. Serve immediately with Green Chili Sauce (page 87).

Serves 4.

CRAB CLAY POT
(Bu Mar Din)

Crab Clay Pot is very easy to prepare. To ensure the finest flavor, live crab should be used if available.

1 live Dungeness crab, 2 to 3 pounds
½ medium yellow onion, sliced
1 large or 2 small stalks lemon grass, crushed and cut into
    4-inch pieces
¾ cup fresh Chicken Stock (page 53)
1 tablespoon Golden Mountain sauce
1 tablespoon bean sauce
1 cup Thai or Italian basil leaves, firmly packed

Soak a clay pot and its cover in water for 1 hour or overnight.
Clean the crab, discarding the top shell, gills, and intestine but saving
    the "butter." Cut the body in half; cut each half into sections with
    2 legs each.
Layer the onion, lemon grass, crab, and crab butter in the clay pot in
    order.
In a bowl combine the Chicken Stock, Golden Mountain sauce, and bean
    sauce. Pour over the ingredients in the clay pot and cover.
Bring to a boil over high heat. Cook for 10 to 15 minutes, until the crab
    is done. Be careful not to overcook. Turn off the heat, add the basil,
    and cover. Serve immediately with Green Chili Sauce (page 87).

Serves 4.

FILET OF FISH CLAY POT
(Bla Mar Din)

Filet of Fish Clay Pot is a quick, easy, mild-flavored dish.

12 to 16 ounces rock cod filet or any firm-fleshed fish
1 medium onion, sliced
1 stalk fresh lemon grass, crushed and cut into 3-inch lengths
50 Thai or Italian basil leaves
½ tablespoon bean sauce
½ cup plus 2 tablespoons fresh Chicken Stock (page 53)

Soak a clay pot and its cover in water for 1 hour or overnight.

Holding the knife at an angle, slice the fish filet into 1-inch pieces. Set aside.

Layer ½ of the onions, all of the lemon grass, and 20 of the basil leaves in the clay pot in order. Add the fish, overlapping the pieces. Top with the remaining onions and basil leaves in order.

In a small bowl combine the bean sauce and Chicken Stock. Pour over the ingredients.

Cover the pot and boil over high heat for 10 to 12 minutes, until the fish is done. The fish should be opaque but still tender and moist. Be careful not to overcook it. Serve immediately with Green Chili Sauce (page 87).

Serves 4 to 6.

Rice and Noodles

 CHILI PEPPER FRIED RICE
(Kow Pat Prik Bai Grapraow)

In Thailand, this dish is made with at least 5 fresh Thai chili peppers, which are crushed with garlic. At the restaurant, dried cayenne and jalapeño chili peppers are combined to put Chili Pepper Fried Rice in the "very hot" category. If holy basil is not available, substitute orange bergamot mint leaves.

> 1 to 2 dried cayenne peppers
> 1 tablespoon oil
> 1 tablespoon minced garlic
> 3 ounces boned, skinned chicken breast, sliced into thin, bite-sized pieces
> 1½ tablespoons oyster sauce
> 2 jalapeño or serrano chili peppers, stems removed, cut length-wise into quarters
> 2 cups cold cooked rice
> 1 tablespoon fish sauce
> ¾ teaspoon sugar
> 20 fresh holy basil or orange bergamot mint leaves
> 3 to 5 sprigs fresh coriander
> 5 cucumber slices, ½ inch thick

Soak the cayenne peppers in hot water for about 15 minutes, until soft. Drain and chop into small pieces. Reserve ¼ teaspoon and set aside.

Heat a well-seasoned pan or wok over high heat and add the oil. When oil is hot, add the garlic and cayenne peppers. Stir-fry until the garlic is light brown.

Add the chicken, oyster sauce, and jalapeño chili peppers in order. Stir-fry for 30 seconds. Add the rice, breaking up any large clumps. Stir-fry for another 45 seconds. Add the fish sauce and sugar and stir-fry for 15 seconds. Add the basil and stir-fry until the leaves are wilted.

Garnish with coriander leaves and cucumber slices. Serve immediately.

Serves 4.

DIVINE RICE WITH PRAWNS OR CRAB
(Kow Pat Gung Bu)

This fried rice dish is very easy to prepare and is typically eaten for lunch. For best results use cold, day-old rice, which won't become soggy when it is cooked a second time. Remember to squeeze the lime over the rice just before eating to enhance the flavors.

> 9 to 12 medium prawns, shelled and deveined (approximately 5 to 8 ounces) *or* 3½ ounces snow crab meat, including legs
> 2 tablespoons oil
> 1 tablespoon minced garlic
> 1½ tablespoons chopped onions
> 1 egg
> 2 cups cold cooked rice
> 6 to 7 teaspoons fish sauce
> ¾ teaspoon sugar
> 1 teaspoon catsup
> ⅛ teaspoon sweet soy sauce
> ¼ wedge tomato, sliced in half at an angle
> 3 to 5 sprigs fresh coriander
> 5 cucumber slices, ½ inch thick
> ½ fresh lime

Using a large strainer to hold the prawns, parboil for 3 seconds until they turn pink on the edges. Be careful not to overcook; the cooking process will be completed later. Drain well and set aside.

Heat a well-seasoned pan or wok over high heat and add the oil. When oil is hot, add the garlic and onions. Stir-fry until light brown.

Crack the egg into the pan and scramble, cooking for about 10 seconds. Add the rice. Stir-fry, breaking up any clumps of rice and the scrambled egg. Add 6 teaspoons of the fish sauce, sugar, catsup, and sweet soy sauce in order. Stir-fry for 30 seconds.

Add the prawns or crab. If using prawns, pour the last teaspoon of fish sauce on the prawns. Stir-fry for another 30 seconds. Add the tomato and stir-fry for 30 seconds, until the prawns are done.

Garnish with the coriander leaves, cucumber slices, and lime. Serve immediately.

Serves 4.

 PEASANT'S RICE
(Kow Pat Gai Mu Nuar)

Peasant's Rice is a mild dish that is very simple to make. Vary it by using pork or beef, instead of chicken. The catsup is added for its smell and color, but should not overpower the fried rice. Squeeze the lime over the dish just before eating.

1 tablespoon oil
1 tablespoon minced garlic
3 to 4 ounces boned, skinned chicken breast, pork, or flank steak, sliced into thin, bite-sized pieces
1 teaspoon oyster sauce
1½ tablespoons chopped onion
1 egg
2 cups cold cooked rice
2 tablespoons fish sauce
¾ teaspoon sugar
1 teaspoon catsup
⅛ teaspoon sweet soy sauce
¼ wedge tomato, sliced in half at an angle
3 to 5 sprigs fresh coriander
5 cucumber slices, ½ inch thick
½ fresh lime

Heat a well-seasoned pan or wok over high heat and add the oil. When oil is hot, add the garlic. Stir-fry until light brown.
Add the chicken, oyster sauce, and chopped onion. Stir-fry for a few seconds. Crack the egg into the pan and scramble, cooking for 10 seconds. Add the rice. Break up any clumps of rice and the scrambled egg. Add the fish sauce, sugar, catsup, sweet soy sauce, and tomato in order. Stir-fry for about 90 seconds.
Garnish with coriander, cucumber slices, and lime. Serve immediately.

Serves 4.

THAI NOODLES
(Phat Thai)

Phat Thai is the most popular noodle dish served at Siam Cuisine. In Thailand, these mild, tangy noodles can be found in any marketplace, so people rarely bother to make them at home. This recipe calls for a pre-made sauce that is combined with the other ingredients in a wok. The sauce will keep in the refrigerator for 1 to 2 months. Bring it to room temperature before using. Just before eating, squeeze the lime over the Phat Thai and mix with the bean sprouts.

Phat Thai Sauce

> 1 ounce preserved tamarind
> 3 tablespoons hot water
> 1½ teaspoons salt
> ½ cup palm sugar
> 6 tablespoons white vinegar
> ¼ to ⅓ cup water

In a small bowl soak the tamarind in the hot water for 30 minutes, until soft. Work the tamarind with your hands for 5 minutes to release the pulp. Press pulp through a strainer. Squeeze out all the liquid and pulp and discard the twigs and seeds. Reserve 1½ tablespoons and set aside.

Place the salt, palm sugar, white vinegar, ¼ cup of the water, and the tamarind in a small saucepan. Place over high heat and start a timer at 10 minutes. Bring to a vigorous boil and lower the heat to medium high. Stir constantly. When the 10 minutes are up, remove the pan from the heat and allow to cool.

The sauce should be the color and consistency of thick, pure maple syrup. If it is too thick, add 2 tablespoons of water and heat slowly over low heat until the water is completely blended. Cook for 2 more minutes. Remove from the heat and cool again. Repeat if necessary.

Makes about ¾ cup.

Phat Thai

        4 ounces dried Jantaboon rice sticks
        Oil for deep-frying
        4 ounces firm tofu, cut into pieces ¾ by 1¼ by 3 inches
        ¼ cup raw peanuts
        1 dried cayenne pepper
        1½ tablespoons oil
        4 teaspoons dried shrimp
        1 teaspoon finely chopped brine-cured radish
        1 teaspoon minced garlic
        1 tablespoon fish sauce
        2½ tablespoons Phat Thai sauce (see above)
        2 green onions, cut into 2-inch lengths
        5 ounces bean sprouts
        ½ fresh lime

Soak the Jantaboon rice sticks in enough cold water to cover for about 30 minutes, until soft. Drain and set aside.

In a deep-fryer, heat the oil to 450°.

Deep-fry the tofu for 3 minutes, until golden brown. Drain on paper towels and allow to cool. Slice ¼ inch thick. Set aside.

Dry-roast the raw peanuts in a wok for 10 minutes at medium-low heat until evenly browned, flipping frequently. Cool to room temperature. In a mortar pound the peanuts into small pieces. Set aside.

Dry-roast the cayenne pepper in the wok over medium heat until it turns a deep red, being careful not to let it burn. In a mortar pound the chili pepper into small flakes. Reserve ¼ teaspoon.

Heat a well-seasoned wok over high heat and add the 1½ tablespoons of oil. When oil is hot, add the dried shrimp. Stir-fry for several seconds. Add the fried tofu, radish, cayenne pepper, and garlic in order. Stir-fry until the garlic is light brown.

Quickly add the rice sticks, fish sauce, and Phat Thai sauce. Stir-fry to completely coat the rice sticks with the sauce. Add the green onions and 2 ounces of the bean sprouts. Stir-fry until heated. Add 2 tablespoons of the crushed peanuts, stir again, and turn off the heat.

Place the Phat Thai on a serving platter. Sprinkle with the rest of the crushed peanuts. Place the remaining bean sprouts and lime to one side of the platter. Serve immediately.

        Serves 4.

BROCCOLI OVER FRESH RICE NOODLES
(Lard Nar)

Lard Nar, fresh rice noodles smothered with a topping, is very popular at the restaurant. Because cooking proceeds quite rapidly, all of the ingredients should be prepared in advance. In Thailand, Lard Nar is eaten at lunchtime and served with pickled chili peppers, which are added according to individual taste. This recipe includes the typical flavor without the chili peppers.

Ingredients for the noodles

½ tablespoon oil
⅛ teaspoon finely chopped garlic
10 ounces fresh rice noodles, separated into individual strands
½ teaspoon sweet soy sauce

Ingredients for the topping

8 ounces broccoli
3½ teaspoons cornstarch
2 tablespoons water
1½ tablespoons oil
½ teaspoon minced garlic
½ tablespoon bean sauce
1 cup plus 2 tablespoons fresh Chicken Stock (page 53)
1¾ tablespoons oyster sauce
1 tablespoon Kwan's Sweet and Sour Sauce (page 87)
½ teaspoon Golden Mountain sauce
⅛ teaspoon sweet soy sauce
6 ounces boned, skinned chicken breast, pork, or flank steak, sliced into thin, bite-sized pieces

To prepare the broccoli, cut the flowers 2½ inches from the top and separate into smaller sections. Peel the stem and cut into rectangular pieces about 3 by 1¼ by 3/16 inches. Blanch the broccoli for about 10 seconds. Drain and set aside.

Combine the cornstarch and water in a small bowl. Set aside.

To cook the noodles, heat a well-seasoned pan over high heat and add the oil. When the oil is hot, add the garlic and stir-fry until light brown. Quickly add the noodles and sweet soy sauce. Gently stir-fry for 2 minutes, until the noodles are hot, being careful not to break them. Transfer to a serving platter and set aside.

To cook the topping, heat the same pan over high heat and add the oil. When oil is hot, add the garlic and bean sauce. Stir-fry until the garlic is light brown.

Add the Chicken Stock, oyster sauce, sweet and sour sauce, Golden Mountain sauce, cornstarch mixture, and sweet soy sauce in order. Stir and bring to a boil to thicken the sauce. Add the chicken and broccoli. Stir-fry for 2 to 3 minutes, until the chicken is done and the broccoli is tender. Pour over the rice noodles and serve immediately.

Serves 2.

NOODLE DELIGHT
(Bamee Lard Nar Gai)

Noodle Delight is a mild-flavored dish. Fresh egg noodles are deep-fried and topped with a variety of ingredients in a thick sweet and sour sauce.

Oil for deep-frying
2 ounces fresh egg noodles
4 teaspoons cornstarch
2 tablespoons water
2 tablespoons oil
1 tablespoon minced garlic
1 tablespoon bean sauce
3 ounces boned, skinned chicken breast, sliced into thin, bite-sized pieces
2 ounces bamboo shoots, thinly sliced
¼ medium yellow onion
3 water chestnuts, sliced
3 to 4 baby corn, cut in half
2 medium mushrooms, sliced
3 tablespoons oyster sauce
1 cup fresh Chicken Stock (page 53)
2 tablespoons Kwan's Sweet and Sour Sauce (page 87)
1 green onion, cut into 2-inch lengths
¼ teaspoon sesame oil

In a deep-fryer, heat the oil to 400°.

Spread the egg noodles loosely in the bottom of the frying basket. Deep-fry for 20 seconds, until golden brown. Drain on paper towels and place on a serving platter. Set aside.

In a small bowl combine the cornstarch and water and set aside.

Heat a well-seasoned pan or wok over high heat and add the 2 table-spoon of oil. When oil is hot, add the garlic and bean sauce. Stir-fry until garlic is light brown.

Add the chicken, bamboo shoots, yellow onion, water chestnuts, baby corn, and mushrooms; stir-fry for several seconds. Add the oyster sauce and Chicken Stock; stir-fry for 1 minute. Add the sweet and sour sauce and cornstarch mixture; stir-fry for 30 seconds. Add the green onion; stir-fry for another 30 seconds. Remove from the heat and add the sesame oil. Pour over the fried noodles and serve immediately.

Serves 4.

FISH CURRY WITH SOMEN NOODLES
(Nam Yah)

Fish Curry is usually eaten for lunch and served in the same manner as Ground Prawn Curry with Somen Noodles. It is medium hot and has a pronounced *krachai* flavor. For convenience, canned tuna is used in this recipe with not too much loss in flavor.

> 7 to 8 ounces dried *somen*
> 2 ounces fresh or frozen *krachai*, thinly sliced (approximately ½ cup)
> 1 to 1½ cups fresh Chicken Stock (page 53)
> 3 tablespoons Basic Curry Paste (page 79)
> 1½ tablespoons ground cayenne pepper
> 5 tablespoons fish sauce
> 5¼ cups thick coconut milk
> 12½-ounce can of tuna in water (reserve the water)
> ½ small shredded cabbage *or* 1½ pounds Blue Lake green beans *or* 1 bitter melon, sliced in half and seeded
> 1 bunch lemon basil (optional)
> 8 ounces bean sprouts (optional)

To prepare the *somen*, follow the instructions given in the recipe for Ground Prawn Curry with Somen Noodles (page 165).

To prepare the fish curry:

Grind the *krachai* in a blender with ½ cup of the Chicken Stock. Place ½ of the mixture in a large well-seasoned pan or wok. Add the curry paste, cayenne pepper, fish sauce, and 2 cups of the coconut milk. Bring to a boil over high heat. Reduce for 15 to 20 minutes, scraping the sides and bottom of the pan, as needed, to prevent sticking or burning.

Tiny pockets of oil from the coconut milk should start to surface at this time. If the oil does not surface, add 3 to 4 tablespoons of Chicken Stock and bring to a boil. Reduce for 4 to 5 minutes. Repeat if necessary.

Cook for another 10 minutes. The curry should have a dark, grainy consistency.

Pound or grind the tuna in a mortar or blender until smooth. If using a blender, add the reserved water from the can. Set aside.

Add the remaining *krachai* mixture, the remaining 3¼ cups of coconut milk, ½ cup of the Chicken Stock, and the tuna and its reserved liquid to the curry. Bring to a boil and remove from heat.

Arrange the cabbage, lemon basil, and bean sprouts on a serving platter. If green beans or bitter melon are used, thinly slice diagonally and blanch for 20 to 30 seconds. Drain and serve with the curry and *somen* bundles.

Serves 6.

PRAWNS WITH COCONUT-FLAVORED RICE NOODLES
(Mee Siam)

Traditionally, the noodles in Mee Siam are served separately from the coconut-flavored sauce. To make sure the proportions are correct for the first-time eater, and for ease of serving at the restaurant, the two parts are combined in the kitchen. Red food coloring is added to the water in which the noodles are soaked, but it is not necessary; it only makes the presentation a little more colorful.

2 ounces dried rice thread or rice stick noodles
⅛ teaspoon red food coloring (optional)
6 to 10 medium prawns, shelled and deveined (approximately
    4 to 7 ounces)
Oil for deep-frying
2 ounces firm tofu, 1 by 1½ by 1½ inches
1 tablespoon oil
2 tablespoons coarsely chopped red onion
1 tablespoon minced garlic
1 tablespoon yellow bean sauce
3 tablespoons thick coconut milk
2 tablespoons Kwan's Sweet and Sour Sauce (page 87)
½ teaspoon sugar
2 ounces bean sprouts
1 green onion, sliced into 2-inch lengths
½ fresh lime

Soak the rice thread noodles in enough cold water to cover. Add the food
    coloring to the soaking water, if desired. When soft, drain and set
    aside.
Using a large strainer to hold the prawns, parboil for 3 seconds until they
    turn pink on the edges. Be careful not to overcook; the cooking
    process will be completed later. Drain well and set aside.
In a deep-fryer, heat the oil to 380°.
Pat the tofu dry and deep-fry for 3 minutes, until golden brown and
    crisp. Cool and slice into pieces ¼ inch thick. Set aside.
Heat a well-seasoned pan or wok over high heat and add the tablespoon
    of oil. When oil is hot, add the red onion, garlic, and yellow bean
    sauce. Stir-fry until the garlic is light brown.
Add the coconut milk and stir-fry for 15 seconds, until blended. Add the
    sweet and sour sauce, sugar, prawns, fried tofu, and rice thread.
    Stir-fry for 30 seconds. Add the bean sprouts and green onion. Stir-
    fry for 2 to 3 minutes, until the prawns are done. Serve immediately
    with the lime.

Serves 4.

GROUND PRAWN CURRY WITH SOMEN NOODLES
(Kanom Jean Nam Prik)

One of the distinguishing features of this medium-hot curry is the use of fresh Kaffir lime juice, which adds a sweet perfume. In Thailand, the curry is served separately from the noodles. Each serving is combined at the table and eaten with a variety of fresh vegetables. The curry can be prepared in advance and kept overnight in the refrigerator. Bring it back to room temperature or warm it up before serving. The *somen* noodles are formed into small bundles and served in a shallow basket to allow the excess water to drain; a colander will do. If Kaffir lime juice is not available, fresh lime juice can be substituted.

> 7 to 8 ounces dried *somen*
> 1½ ounces preserved tamarind
> 6 tablespoons hot water
> Roots and stems of 4 whole, medium coriander plants (discard leaves or use in another recipe)
> 1½ cups water
> 15 medium prawns, shelled and deveined (approximately 8 ounces)
> 6 tablespoons peeled, split mung beans
> 3 dried cayenne peppers
> 4 tablespoons raw peanuts
> 3 tablespoons oil
> 2 tablespoons thinly sliced shallots, firmly packed
> 1 tablespoon thinly sliced garlic, firmly packed
> 4½ tablespoons fish sauce
> 4 tablespoons palm sugar
> 1¾ cups thick coconut milk
> 2 to 2½ tablespoons fresh lime juice (save rind)
> 2 to 2¼ tablespoons fresh Kaffir lime juice (save rind)
> 1 bunch Chinese watercress leaves, cleaned *or* ½ small cabbage, shredded *or* 1 pound Blue Lake green beans *or* petals from 1 banana bud, sliced and steamed
> 6 to 8 dried Thai chili peppers (optional)

To prepare the *somen*:
Boil a large pot of water. Add the *somen* and bring the water back to a

boil. Boil for 3 minutes, until tender. Drain and rinse with cold water to stop the cooking process.

To form the bundles, place a small amount of the cooked *somen* in a medium bowl of water. Work with a little at a time to prevent the *somen* from absorbing too much water and becoming soggy. Drape enough *somen* over your index finger to cover it, allowing the loose strands to hang in front of the other fingers. Arrange the strands so that they all fall in the same direction, dipping the *somen* back in the water if necessary. Fold up the loose ends to form a rectangular bundle; place in a shallow basket or colander. Repeat the process for the remaining *somen*, arranging the bundles in a circular pattern around the basket. Set aside.

To prepare the Ground Prawn Curry:

In a small bowl soak the tamarind in the hot water for 30 minutes, until soft. Work the tamarind with your hands for 10 minutes to release the pulp. Press the pulp through a strainer. Squeeze out all the liquid and pulp and discard the twigs and seeds. Reserve 3 tablespoons and set aside.

Place the coriander and water in a small saucepan and bring to a boil. Add the prawns and cook for 1 minute. Remove the prawns, reserving the water they were cooked in. Set the coriander and the prawn water aside. In a mortar or blender pound or grind the prawns into small pieces. Remove and set aside.

In a mortar pound the coriander stems and roots to a fine paste. Remove and set aside.

In a skillet dry-roast the mung beans over medium-high heat until browned, flipping frequently to brown evenly. In a blender grind the beans into very fine pieces. Remove and set aside.

Dry-roast the cayenne peppers in the skillet over medium heat until they are deep red, being careful not to let them burn. Place them in a mortar and crush into small flakes. Reserve 2 teaspoons.

Dry-roast the peanuts in the skillet for 10 minutes over medium heat until evenly browned, flipping frequently. Allow to cool. In the mortar pound the peanuts to a lumpy paste almost the consistency of chunky peanut butter. Remove and set aside.

Heat a well-seasoned pan over medium-high heat and add 2 tablespoons of the oil. When oil is hot, add the shallots and sauté until dark brown, being careful not to let them burn. Remove and set aside.

Using the same oil, sauté the garlic over medium heat until dark brown, being careful not to let it burn. Remove and set aside.

Reserve 1½ tablespoons of the browning oil in the pan. Add the cayenne peppers, 1 tablespoon of the fish sauce, and ½ tablespoon of the palm sugar. Sauté over medium heat for 3 minutes, until the chili peppers become a deep, dark red. Stir constantly to prevent burning. Remove from heat and set aside.

In a large saucepan combine the coconut milk, the remaining 3½ tablespoons of the fish sauce, the remaining 3½ tablespoons of the palm sugar, coriander, tamarind, and mung beans. Add the water the prawns were cooked in plus enough additional water to total 1⅔ cups. Bring to a vigorous boil over high heat. Turn off the heat.

Add the prawns, peanuts, shallots, garlic, and oil-cayenne mixture. Stir, breaking up any lumps. Add the lime juices and rinds and stir again. Pour into a serving dish and allow to cool slightly before serving. Remove the rinds after 10 to 15 minutes to prevent the sauce from getting bitter.

Arrange the vegetables on a platter and serve with the curry and *somen* bundles. If green beans are used, thinly slice diagonally and blanch for 20 to 30 seconds. Rinse with cold water, drain, and serve.

Using 1 tablespoon of the oil, fry the Thai chili peppers (if desired) in a skillet over medium heat until deep red, being careful not to let them burn. Serve with the vegetables.

Serves 4.

Desserts

 ## STEAMED COCONUT CUSTARD
(Sang Kaya)

This light and fluffy custard is often served over Sweet Rice in Cream of Coconut (page 170). It is usually made much sweeter, but this is how Somchai and Kwan like to prepare it at home.

½ cup palm sugar
½ teaspoon salt
2⅜ cups thick coconut milk
3 large or 4 small eggs, lightly beaten

In a medium saucepan combine the palm sugar, salt, and coconut milk. Bring to a boil over high heat. Lower the heat to medium high and reduce for 30 minutes, until approximately 1 cup remains. Stir constantly to prevent burning, and do not allow the mixture to boil over. (If it does, start over since the oil from the coconut milk will be lost.) Cool slightly so that the eggs do not set when added.
Gradually add the eggs, using a wire whisk to blend thoroughly.
Pour the custard into an 8-inch square baking pan or deep bowl that will fit in your steamer. Place the baking dish in the steamer and steam for about 50 minutes. Check for doneness by inserting a knife into the custard. If it comes out clean, the custard is done. Allow to cool. Serve over sweet rice.

Serves 6.

SWEET RICE IN CREAM OF COCONUT
(Kow Neow)

Sweet Rice in Cream of Coconut is eaten with Coconut Custard (page 169), Black Beans (page 171), or sliced mango. To keep it from burning and becoming soggy, the rice is soaked overnight, drained, and steamed in a bamboo basket. The cooking time will vary with each crop, but always use the best grade possible for desserts. If available, use Thai sweet rice instead of the Japanese variety. Sweet Rice in Cream of Coconut may be kept overnight, but do not refrigerate it or the grains will become dry and hard.

> 2 cups uncooked Thai sweet rice
> 4¾ cups thick coconut milk
> ½ cup sugar
> 2 teaspoons salt

To wash the rice, place it in a bowl and add enough water to cover. Rub the grains between your palms several times. This will make the rice shine when cooked. Drain and replace the water. Repeat 2 or 3 times, until the water runs clear.

Soak the rice overnight in enough water to cover. If using Japanese sweet rice, soak for 2 hours.

To cook the sweet rice, drain it into a bamboo basket or a cloth-lined colander. Place the basket over a pot filled with enough boiling water to steam the rice. Make sure the water does not touch the basket. Cover the rice and steam over high heat for 15 minutes. Remove the cover and flip the rice in the basket once so that it will cook evenly. It will appear to be one big ball. Replace the cover and cook for another 10 minutes, until the rice is done. If the rice is done before the cream of coconut is completed, drain the water from the steamer and replace the basket. Set aside.

While the rice is cooking, combine the coconut milk, sugar, and salt in a medium saucepan. Bring to a boil over high heat. Lower to medium-high and reduce for 20 to 30 minutes, until about 1 cup remains. Stir constantly to prevent burning, and do not allow the mixture to boil over. (If it does, start over since the oil from the coconut milk will be lost.) Remove from the stove.

Add the sweet rice. Stir for several minutes, until the liquid is absorbed.

Cover the rice and let it stand for 10 to 20 minutes. Serve at room temperature.

Serves 4 to 6.

 ## BLACK BEANS
(Tua Dum)

This is a wonderfully warming dessert to be eaten alone or as a topping for sweet rice, custard, or sliced mango. It consists of whole black beans floating in a bath of sweetened coconut milk. The finished dessert can be kept in the refrigerator for up to 5 days; add 2 tablespoons of water before reheating.

> 8 ounces dried black beans
> 10 ounces palm sugar
> 2⅝ cups thick coconut milk
> ½ cup water
> ½ teaspoon salt

Soak the black beans overnight in enough water to cover.

Rinse the beans several times, removing any foreign matter. Put them in a pot with enough water to cover. Boil over medium-high heat for about 1 hour, until well done. Drain and set aside.

Place the palm sugar, coconut milk, water, and salt in a medium saucepan. Bring to a boil over high heat. Stir until the sugar has dissolved. Add the black beans and bring to a boil again. Do not allow the mixture to boil over. Remove from heat and cool slightly.

Serve warm over sweet rice, custard, or sliced mango.

Serves 6 to 8.

 ## COCONUT PUDDING
(Thago)

Each bite of this Coconut Pudding is filled with crunchy slices of water chestnut. In Thailand, it is served in a banana-leaf cup and is topped with a thin layer of sweetened coconut milk. Do not overcook the pudding. It should be opaque and not clear. If it becomes clear, start over. The pudding can be kept in the refrigerator for up to 2 days.

Pudding

    ½ cup rice flour
    2 cups water
    ½ cup sliced water chestnuts
    ⅓ cup brown sugar, packed
    ¼ cup white sugar
    6 small red rose petals

Topping

    1 cup thick coconut milk
    1 tablespoon sugar
    ¼ teaspoon salt

To make the pudding:

In a small bowl combine the rice flour and ½ cup of the water; set aside.

In a small saucepan combine the water chestnuts, brown sugar, white sugar, and remaining 1½ cups of water. Bring to a boil over medium-high heat, then lower heat to medium.

Slowly stir in ½ cup of the rice-flour mixture with a wire whisk. Reserve the remaining rice-flour mixture for the topping. Whisk for about a minute and remove from the stove. The pudding should still be opaque. Makes about 1½ cups.

Spoon about ¼ cup of the pudding into each of 6 two-ounce dessert cups, filling them to ¼ inch below the rim. Smooth the surface and set aside.

To make the topping:

Combine the coconut milk, sugar, and salt in a small saucepan. Bring to a boil over medium-high heat, being careful not to let it burn. Slowly stir in the reserved rice-flour mixture to thicken slightly. Remove from heat.

Pour 2 tablespoons of the topping over the pudding, filling the dessert cups to the rim. Garnish with rose petals.

    Makes 6.

BAKED MUNG BEAN CUSTARD
(Kanom Mar Gang Tua)

Baked Mung Bean Custard is baked and then topped with sautéed shallots. It may sound strange, but it actually makes a very interesting and tasty combination. It's one of those things that just has to be tried!

> ½ cup peeled, split mung beans
> 2 cups water
> ¼ cup white sugar
> ½ cup palm sugar
> ½ teaspoon salt
> 2⅜ cups thick coconut milk
> 3 large eggs, lightly beaten
> 2 tablespoons oil
> 3 tablespoons thinly sliced shallots, firmly packed

In a small bowl soak the mung beans in enough water to cover. Allow to stand for at least 2 hours or overnight.

Drain the mung beans and boil in 2 cups water for 15 to 20 minutes, until tender. Drain and place in a blender and set aside.

In a medium saucepan combine the white sugar, palm sugar, salt, and coconut milk. Reduce over high heat, stirring constantly, for 30 minutes, until about 1 cup remains. Do not allow the mixture to boil over. (If it does, start over since the oil from the coconut milk will be lost.) Cool and add to the blender.

Grind the ingredients until the mung beans are pureed. Gradually add the eggs and blend. Pour the batter into an 8-inch square baking pan.

Preheat the oven to 350° and bake the custard for 30 minutes, until golden brown. Test for doneness by inserting a toothpick into the custard; if it comes out clean, the custard is done.

While the custard bakes, heat a well-seasoned pan over medium-high heat and add the oil. When oil is hot, add the shallots and sauté until golden brown. Pour the shallots and oil over the custard and bake for another 4 minutes. Remove from the oven and cool to room temperature.

To serve, cut into 1½-inch squares.

Makes 25 pieces.

THAI-STYLE GARLIC COOKIE
(Grob Kem)

These "cookies" are actually deep-fried wonton skins glazed with a peppery, garlicky, sugar coating. Kwan made these as a child and sold them in the marketplace to get extra spending money. The glaze should be soft and slightly sticky, not brittle. These cookies can be served as a dessert or as a snack.

> Oil for deep-frying
> 30 thick wonton skins, cut in half diagonally and separated (20
>   skins per inch)
> 8 ounces brown sugar
> 2 tablespoons water
> ¼ to ⅓ cup garlic, crushed and minced
> 35 small marshmallows
> 1 tablespoon fish sauce
> 1 to 1½ teaspoons ground white pepper
> ¼ cup fresh coriander roots, loosely packed

In a deep-fryer, heat the oil to 380°.

Place one layer of wonton skins in the bottom of the frying basket. Fry for about 1½ minutes, turning to brown both sides. The skins will puff up immediately and rise to the surface. Separate them if necessary. Remove from oil and drain on paper towels. Repeat for the remaining wonton skins, reheating oil to 380° each time. Spread wonton skins out on a roasting pan and set aside.

In a small saucepan dissolve the brown sugar in the water. Add the minced garlic, marshmallows, fish sauce, white pepper, and coriander roots. Boil over medium-high heat until the marshmallows melt. Cook for 3 to 4 minutes, stirring constantly to prevent sticking or burning.

To test for doneness, allow the sauce to drip from the spoon and cool slightly. If it is sticky to the touch, almost forming threads, it is ready. Remove from the stove and pour over the deep-fried wonton skins, mixing gently to coat evenly.

Makes 60.

STEAMED TAPIOCA CAKE
(Kanom Chan)

Steamed Tapioca Cake is a soft, gelatinous "cake" that is steamed in layers. To make it "look pretty," food coloring is added to alternate layers. Kwan prefers to use canned "cream of coconut for piña colada" in this recipe to give the cake a different flavor and aroma. If not available, reduce a mixture of 3½ cups of thick coconut milk and 1 cup of sugar by half over a medium-high heat.

> 4½ cups tapioca flour or starch (approximately 16 ounces)
> ¾ cup sugar
> ½ teaspoon salt
> 15-ounce can cream of coconut for piña colada
> 2⅝ cups thick coconut milk
> ¼ teaspoon red or green food coloring

Combine the tapioca flour, sugar, salt, and cream of coconut in a large bowl. Using your hands, knead the batter to remove any lumps. Add 1 cup of the coconut milk and knead until thoroughly combined. Add the remaining 1⅝ cups coconut milk; mix well. The batter should be silky and relatively loose, running off your hands in ribbons. Makes about 6 cups of batter.

Divide the batter in half. Add the food coloring to one half and blend thoroughly.

Place an 8-inch square cake pan in a large steamer. Starting with the uncolored batter, pour about ⅔ cup into the cake pan. Steam, covered, for 12 to 15 minutes, until the layer becomes transparent and very shiny. Repeat, alternating the colored and uncolored batters, ending with a colored layer on top. Occasionally check the water level in the bottom of the steamer and replenish with more boiling water if necessary. Steam for another 10 minutes. Remove from the steamer and cool.

To serve, cut into 2-inch squares.

Makes 16 pieces.

SWEET RICE CUSTARD CAKE
(Kanom Bah Bin)

Sweet Rice Custard Cake is baked until the bottom and top crusts are dark brown. The interior is loaded with coconut flakes and is both crunchy and chewy in texture. Use any combination of fresh, frozen, or dried unsweetened coconut flakes.

1 egg
3 cups sugar
7 tablespoons soft butter
3½ cups thick coconut milk
4½ cups sweet rice flour (approximately 16 ounces)
½ cup rice flour
5 cups unsweetened coconut flakes

In a large bowl combine the egg, sugar, 6 tablespoons of the butter, and the coconut milk. Gradually add the sweet rice flour and rice flour, blending well after each addition. Add the coconut flakes and mix into the batter.

Preheat oven to 350°.

Coat the bottom and sides of a baking pan, 9 by 13 inches, with the remaining tablespoon of butter. Pour the batter into the pan and bake for 80 minutes, until the cake is dark brown on top. Remove from oven and cool to room temperature.

To serve, cut into 2-inch squares.

Makes 24 pieces.

Sources for Thai Ingredients

If there is a Southeast Asian or Thai market in your area, you will probably be able to obtain most of the Thai ingredients called for in this cookbook. The following list contains the addresses and phone numbers of stores in several large cities of the United States.

CALIFORNIA,
San Francisco Bay Area

Chao Thai Market
2442 San Pablo Avenue
Berkeley, California 94702
415-486-0515

A-Thai Market
259 Tenth Street
Oakland, California 94607
415-834-3333

New Saigon Market
441 - 443 Ninth Street
Oakland, California 94607
415-839-4149

Bangkok Grocery
3236 Geary Boulevard
San Francisco, California 94118
415-221-5863

May Wah Trading Company
1230 Stockton Street
San Francisco, California 94133
415-648-8686

CALIFORNIA, Central Valley

Mekong Oriental Supermarket
1301 Broadway
Sacramento, California 95818
916-446-7243

CALIFORNIA, Los Angeles Area

Bangkok Market
4757 Melrose Avenue
Los Angeles, California 90029
213-662-9705

Thai Market
10455 Mills Avenue
Montclair, California 91763
714-621-4472

Thai Number One Market
5927 Cherry Avenue
North Long Beach, California 90805
213-422-6915

Tomlinson's Nurseries
11758 East Whittier Boulevard
Whittier, California 90601

213-698-5778
213-698-5221
(Kaffir lime trees, potted herbs, holy basil)

COLORADO

Thai Binh Market
1445 Dayton
Denver, Colorado 80231
303-344-4126

Thai Grocery 1
1001 South Federal Boulevard
Denver, Colorado 80219
303-935-7426

FLORIDA

Trung My
8737 South West 72nd Street
Miami, Florida 33173
305-279-9943

Asian Market
3214 Ninth Street North
St. Petersburgh, Florida 33704
813-822-6110

Thai Market
3323-25 South Dale Mabry
Highway
Tampa, Florida 33609
813-837-5735

HAWAII

Siam General Store
171 North Beretania
Honolulu, Hawaii 96817
808-533-3784

ILLINOIS

AA Siam Grocery
1053 West Granville
Chicago, Illinois 60660
312-262-2686

Bangkok Grocery
1003-5 West Leland Avenue
Chicago, Illinois 60640
312-784-0001

Thai Grocery
5014-5016 North Broadway Avenue
Chicago, Illinois 60640
312-561-5354

Thai Market
3920 North Broadway
Chicago, Illinois 60613
312-477-3910

Thai Oriental Market
1656 East 55th Street
Chicago, Illinois 60615
312-324-8714

NEW YORK

Bangkok Market
805-809 Driggs Avenue
Brooklyn, New York 11211
718-384-1188

Bangkok Market
106 Park Street
New York, New York 10013
212-349-1979

Bangkok Village Grocery, Inc.
206 Thompson
New York, New York 10012
212-777-9272

Thailand Food Corporation
2445 Broadway
New York, New York 10024
212-799-5739

TEXAS

Tan Viet Market
10315 Ferguson Drive
Dallas, Texas 75228
214-324-5160

Thailand Market
2216 West Grauwyler Road
Dallas, Texas 75228
214-986-5855

Truong Nguyen Market
205 Village Plaza
Dallas, Texas 75042
214-276-1185

Bangkok Market
3404 Navigation
Houston, Texas 77003
713-223-8303

Hoa Binh Supermarket
2800 Travis Street
Houston, Texas 77006
713-520-9558

Viet Ho Supermarket
8200 Wilcrest
Houston, Texas 77072
713-561-8706

Vietnam Plaza, Inc.
2200 Jefferson Street
Houston, Texas 77003
713-222-0731
713-222-6280

WASHINGTON

Asian Connection
409 Maynard Avenue South
Seattle, Washington 98104
206-587-6010

Rainier Oriental
2919 Rainier Avenue South
Seattle, Washington 98144
206-721-0899

Saigon Market
1034 South Jackson Street
Seattle, Washington 98104
206-322-5622

Viet Hoa Market
676 South Jackson Street
Seattle, Washington 98104
206-621-8499

Somchai Aksomboon and his wife, Kwanruan, owners of Siam Cuisine, were raised in the countryside outside Bangkok. Both their parents were merchants—Kwan's family sold fruits and vegetables. In 1972 Chai came to the University of Texas at Arlington to study mechanical engineering. As he was opening his first Thai restaurant, he met Kwan, who had come to the United States with her two children.

Kwan rarely cooked in Thailand; it was always her mother or father who prepared the meals. But when she found no Thai cooking in America, she wrote home for recipes. Her mother sent lists of ingredients without the exact proportions. Kwan learned how to make each dish by trial and error from her memory of what the food should taste like. Chai has credited the rich flavorings of Siam Cuisine's vegetarian dishes with the fact that three months of the year his mother cooked only non-meat dishes as part of Buddhist observances. The Aksomboons came to the San Francisco Bay Area in 1975 and worked at several restaurants before opening Siam Cuisine in 1978. Their children have grown up in the restaurant, waiting on tables and bussing dishes, contributing to its growing reputation as a leading Thai restaurant in the San Francisco Bay Area.

Diana Hiranaga performed the task of writing down ingredients and cooking methods into recipes appropriate for the home kitchen. She tested the recipes, taking samples back to Siam Cuisine for "taste tests" and recommended adjustments by Kwan and Chai, the proprietors of Siam Cuisine. As she says in the preface: "I went back to my kitchen and made the recipe again, repeating the whole process until the flavors were just right." She was performing a task of transposing, since the dishes did after all originate in home kitches. Diana was born in Stockton of a farming family who opened a Japanese/American grocery store with three other families when she was a young child. She graduated from the University of California, is the mother of a four-year-old and plays the Japanese *shamisen*, a stringed folk instrument. She has traveled extensively in Thailand and the Far East. For the last four years she has studied Thai cooking with Chai and Kwan, and has devised several special dishes for the Siam Cuisine.